75¢

D0706847

The Explosive
Double Slot
Offense

Tom F. Smythe, MA
Head Football Coach
Lewis & Clark College
Portland, Oregon

Leisure Press
Champaign, Illinois

Library of Congress Cataloging-in-Publication Data

Smythe, Tom F., 1940–
   The explosive double slot offense / Tom F. Smythe.
      p.   cm.
   ISBN 0-88011-303-0
   1. Football—Offense. 2. Football—Coaching. I. Title.
GV951.8.S65   1988   87-31850
796.332'2—dc19   CIP

Developmental Editor: Judy Patterson Wright, PhD
Production Director: Ernie Noa
Projects Manager: Lezli Harris
Copy Editor: Claire Mount
Assistant Editors: Christine Drews and JoAnne Hutchcraft Cline
Proofreader: Jane Clapp
Typesetter: Sonnie Bowman
Text Design: Keith Blomberg
Text Layout: Keith Blomberg
Cover Design: Jack Davis
Cover Photo: Focus West
Illustrations By: William R. Eckmann
Printed By: Braun-Brumfield

ISBN: 0-88011-303-0

Printed in the United States of America

10 9 8 7 6 5 4 3 2 1

Leisure Press
A Division of Human Kinetics Publishers, Inc.
Box 5076, Champaign, IL 61820
1-800-342-5457
1-800-334-3665 (in Illinois)

To Don Kieling, my teacher, coach, colleague, and friend. Without his trust, guidance, advice, and loyalty, I would not be where I am today. Also, to the players at Lakeridge High School, without whose ability and talent I would not have had an opportunity to achieve success.

Acknowledgments

I want to thank Evelyn Matthews, who was always there when I needed something done and was always willing to help, and Robin Morse, who did all the typing with such enthusiasm and good humor.

I am also grateful to the following football coaches from whom I learned all my football and to whom I attribute my philosophy of both football and life:

Cliff Giffin, Lake Oswego High School, 1956–1957
Vince Dulcich, Lake Oswego High School, 1958
Brad Eklund, University of Oregon, 1959
John Robinson, University of Oregon, 1959
Doug Scovil, College of San Mateo, 1960
Joe Huston, Lewis & Clark College, 1962–1964
Fred Wilson, Lewis & Clark College, 1962–1964
Gleason Eakin, Willamina High School, 1965
Choctaw Smith, Willamina High School, 1966
Ron Parrish, Tigard High School, 1967–1968
Boyd Crawford, Lake Oswego High School, 1969
Craig Fertig, Oregon State University, 1978

Contents

Preface

I have often been asked for written information about our version of the double slot offense. I have sent information about our offense to high school coaches from Florida to Texas as well as college coaches from Oregon State University to the University of Pittsburgh. In response to these many inquiries I have written *The Explosive Double Slot Offense.* Although many offensive football books have been written over the years, most of these, with the exception of Tiger Ellison's original book on the run and shoot, have not provided specific information concerning this wide-open style of offensive football.

The Explosive Double Slot Offense covers almost every detail of our offense, from the organization of practices to the integral parts of each play. I have not included the subject of line blocking techniques, which could take up a book by itself. It is my hope that this book will provide up-to-date information that will be invaluable to coaches of all levels, from the new head coach to the old-timer, who are interested in the wide-open offense of the future.

I have included information gained from seventeen years as a head coach as well as from my experience as a major college and professional assistant coach. It is my hope that this book will serve as a guide for those coaches at all levels who are interested in this offensive system.

How the Double Slot Can Help You

This is a book about offense, a wide-open and exciting offense. The idea that the best offense is a good defense is *not* our belief; rather, we believe that the best offense is a good offense! This offense has proven itself to be highly explosive and imaginative over the years. This book will help revitalize your offense and give it some explosive, big-play potential!

Develop More Offense

There are really only two offensive theories. The first is to keep it simple; run only a few plays, and run them well (a small bag of tricks, so to speak). The Vince Lombardi Green Bay Packers were a great example of this theory. The second theory, and the one we believe in, is never to have an empty bag. If the basic plays aren't working, reach into the bag and pull something out. A change of formation, an unexpected motion, or a trick play may change the tempo of the game in your favor. In other words, don't have a small bag of tricks. Don't have a grab bag, but have a varied attack. This book will help you expand your offense and give it flexibility. The combination pass patterns, goal line pass offense, and run blocking schemes will be of particular value.

Teach in a Simple Manner

Football is a simple game. Even the most complicated sets of formations, motions, patterns, and plays can be taught in a simple, logical manner. Don't sell the players short; they can handle whatever is given to them as long as it is planned carefully and taught well. Don't make the mistake of saying, "This is really difficult, so pay attention," or believing coaches who say, "This is so tough you can't do anything else," or "Concentrate all your time on this or that, you can't do both." If you tell kids it's tough, they will believe you. If you don't tell them it's tough, they will think it's easy and it will be!

A good example of this is the beginning golfer. One pro says "Keep your left arm straight, keep your head down, bend your left knee first, rotate your hips, keep your hands high, take the club straight back, hit through the ball, shift your weight to the left side on the downswing, and follow through." The result is that the player is so confused he can't hit the ball. Another pro says, "Hit the ball forward!" Then they work on things one at a time. Football can be taught just as easily, one thing at a time!

Add Diversity

Above all, use imagination in your offense. Don't be afraid to fool with a new play in practice. If it doesn't work, throw it out. Don't be afraid to adopt something you have seen on TV or something that an opponent has used against you. No one's offense is entirely his own. The best offense is the one that will be able to take advantage of what the defense gives it. For example, we have always been known as a passing team, and we will throw the ball at any time; however, most years we have gained more yards rushing than passing. In other words, if the defense plays the pass, be able to run and vice versa.

Add Flexibility

The basic double slot has nearly always been our entire offense. Each year our emphasis is a little different depending on our personnel. Some years, for example, the fullback will be the best running back, so we will run a lot of fullback pitch, draw-trap, and inside veer. If the slotbacks are the best runners, we will run more buck-sweep and counter. Change the emphasis but not the thrust of the offense. Be flexible enough to take advantage of the abilities of your players. Give them a chance for success. Don't ask them to do something they can't do. Use your personnel to its best advantage; don't change your entire offense each year, but do change the emphasis to suit the best abilities of your players.

In writing this book, I did not mean for coaches to apply it, word for word, to their offense. We never have the entire offense in at one time, only that part which the kids can handle and do best. However, I hope that, by presenting the entire offense, I can help you use parts of it in your own scheme. It may spark enough interest so that you will begin using your imagination to improve your own offense.

Periodically I will refer to past successes at Lakeridge High School, Lake Oswego, Oregon. This is not done to impress anyone with statistics or to infer that we have all the answers, but simply to give credence to the play, drill, technique, idea, or thought. I ask you to forgive me this slight indulgence.

One last thing: Please understand that this is only one offense. It is not the *only* offense. We happen to believe in the wide-open type offense. If you decide to use just one idea or play from the book, and it works for you, *The Explosive Double Slot Offense* will have served its purpose.

Chapter

1

Installing the Double Slot

You should approach each year as though you were putting in a completely new offense. Begin with the huddle and work through alignment and stance, cadence, formations, adjustments, terminology, and motion. Chapter 1 covers the basics as they are taught at Lakeridge High School.

The Huddle

In the choir huddle the quarterback faces the line of scrimmage and the other ten players face the quarterback (Diagram 1.1).

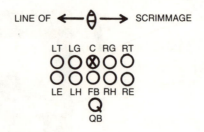

Diagram 1.1   The Huddle

The quarterback receives the play from the sideline (by either signal or messenger) and sets the huddle by saying, "Ready-set." At this time the row of linemen stands at attention, with hands on hips, and the backs and ends snap to position with hands on knees. Both rows of players look directly at the quarterback. The verbal sequence by the quarterback is formation, motion, play, and snap count. Example: "10, Red, Sweep Right, on Hike."

After calling the play the quarterback then says, "Center." The center and both split ends break the huddle and head to the line of scrimmage. All other players turn and face the line of scrimmage. The quarterback then says, "Ready-break." The remaining players then clap hands in unison and jog to their positions.

Alignments and Stance

Specific alignments and stance need to be adjusted according to the position played.

Split End

The normal alignment is an eight- to ten-yard split from the offensive tackle. When restricted by the sideline, never align closer than four yards from the sideline. In normal field positions, when in doubt, take a wider split. The receivers assume a sprinter's stance, with slightly bent knees and waist, the head over the front foot, and the inside foot back. The arms hang relaxed and motionless, outside the knees. The receiver looks in at the ball and is ready to move as the ball is snapped rather than on the snap count, as it is often too difficult to hear the quarterback's cadence. Although a three-point stance allows for a quicker release, the advantage of better vision in a two-point stance is more important. Because most teams are right-handed, we place the bigger or better blocker on the right side, especially in the run game. We like to place the faster end on the left side because big play throwback routes seem to be more successful when the quarterback sprints to his right.

Slotbacks

The normal alignment is three yards outside and one yard off the butt of the tackle. The alignment is of course adjusted for various plays. The slotbacks assume a three-point stance, with their inside foot back and their inside hand down. The left half is therefore in a right-handed stance and the right half is in a left-handed stance. It is much easier to go in motion from this position.

> *Note:* **Put the best runner at left half and the best receiver at right half. Always place a left-handed player at the right slot. It is more natural for left-handed players to run to their left and right-handed players to their right.**

Fullback

The fullback aligns his hand three yards from the quarterback's feet. Adjust the alignment, forward or back, according to his speed. Use a three-point stance for the fullback, and allow him to assume his natural right- or left-handed stance.

> *Note:* **Your best blocker should be at fullback, regardless of his size.**

The backs assume a basic heel-to-toe foot relationship and put the fingertips of their down hand on the ground. The up forearm should rest on the knee. The weight should be evenly distributed on the balls of the feet, and there should be a slight forward lean, not enough to put pressure on the fingers. From this stance it is much easier to move sideways for motion or play action.

Quarterback

The quarterback assumes a fairly tall stance with only a slight bend at the knees. His feet should be parallel, shoulder-width apart, and his arms at nearly a forty-five-degree angle with his hands under the center. This allows him to move right or left with equal ability.

Cadence

The cadence is as follows: Set-*Go*; Ready-*Hike*. The ball is snapped on either "Go" or "Hike." For plays with no motion, the word *go* is the snap count. For plays with motion, the word *hike* is the snap count.

Set-Go is a rhythmic cadence. It helps to draw out the word *set.* Tell the quarterback to say it as if it were two words, "Say-*et*," then emphasize "go." Example: "Say-*et*" (pause), "Go." Hike is the nonrhythmic snap count. When the quarterback uses the word *ready,* the players are alerted to the impending snap count. For plays using motion, the motion back will leave on the word *go.* The longer the motion, the longer the pause between "Go" and "Ready-Hike."

Formations

Numbers are used for formations. Names are used for all patterns as well as to describe running plays and action. The first digit stands for the formation (Diagrams 1.2 through 1.9).

> *Note:* **On all formations we use a standard rule for line splits. Start with a three-foot split and reduce to two only if necessary.**

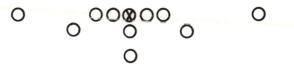

Diagram 1.2   "1" Double Slot Set

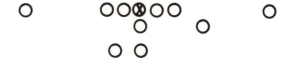

Diagram 1.3   "2" Two Back Set: Slot Right (Tailback at LH on 2 and 3)

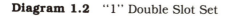

Diagram 1.4   "3" Two Back Set, Slot Left

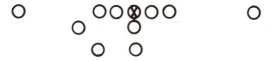

Diagram 1.5   "4" Two Back Set, Slot Right (TB at RH on 4 and 5)

Diagram 1.6   "5" Two Back Set, Slot Left

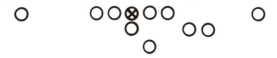

Diagram 1.7   "6" Overload Right

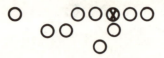

Diagram 1.8   "7" Overload Left

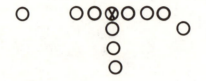

Diagram 1.9   "8" Short Yardage Set

Adjustments

By using three basic adjustments you can create many different formations. These simple adjustments allow greater flexibility in offensive sets.

Tight End

A triple-digit number puts the slot on the formation side on the line of scrimmage (Diagram 1.10).

Diagram 1.10   "100"

In the two back sets it may be beneficial to designate one slot as the running back (tailback) and one as the slot (or tight end) (Diagram 1.11).

> *Note:* **It is necessary for the split end on the side of the tight end to move off the line of scrimmage to the flanker position.**

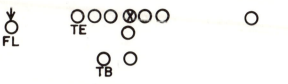

Diagram 1.11   "300"

Wide

Another adjustment in alignment is to move the slotback to a different width. The wide adjustment puts the slotback halfway between the split end and the offensive tackle (Diagrams 1.12 and 1.13).

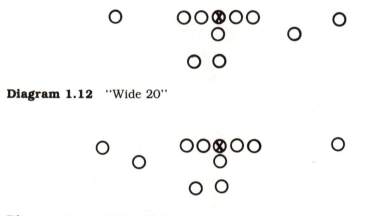

Diagram 1.12   "Wide 20"

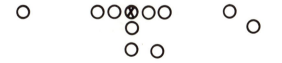

Diagram 1.13   "Wide 30"

Twins

The twins adjustment puts the slotback outside the split end (Diagrams 1.14 and 1.15).

By using these small adjustments you can quickly and very simply alter the look of the double slot formation.

Diagram 1.14   "Twins 40"

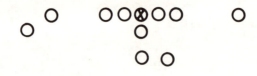

Diagram 1.15   "Twins 50"

Terminology

The second digit stands for run (0), play action pass (6 and 7), or drop back pass (8 and 9). Even numbers are passes with action to the right, and odd numbers signify pass action to the left (Diagrams 1.16 to 1.18).

Diagram 1.16   "10 Rip, Belly Right"

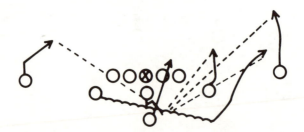

Diagram 1.17   "16 Rip, Belly Right, Hot Pass Right"

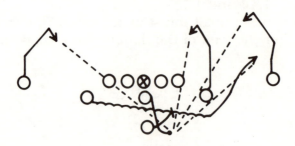

Diagram 1.18   "18 Rip, First Down, LH Flood"

Motion

We use motion to gain an advantage. If the defense ignores the motion, we have gained a numerical advantage; if the defense rotates toward the motion, it will create a one-on-one coverage away from the motion. Motion can be deceptive and create doubt in the minds of the defensive backs. At the very least it causes the opponents to spend more time with their defensive game plan (Diagrams 1.19 to 1.21).

> *Note:* **Flash motion goes toward the play; flash-away motion goes away from the play.**

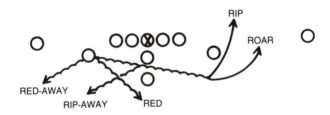

Diagram 1.19   Left Half Motion

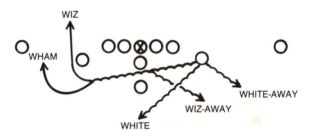

Diagram 1.20   Right Half Motion

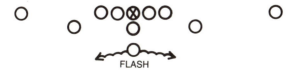

Diagram 1.21   Fullback Motion

Chapter 2

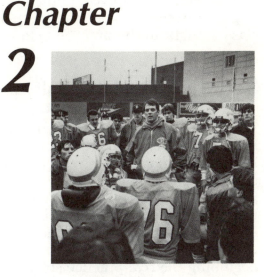

Practice Organization

This chapter describes exactly how to organize practices including warm-up time, kicking game, offensive and defensive isolation time, and team play.

The basic concept is to combine individual practice time for each position with enough group and team practice time to cover all areas of the game. Each coach works with a particular position, for all age groups. This not only allows each coach more time to work with and get to know the younger players, but also gives those players the benefit of working with the same coach for their entire careers. In addition, by being in the same drill as the varsity starters, the younger players can learn firsthand by watching the older players up close.

Each practice begins exactly twenty minutes after the last class of the day. This leaves no time for the players to waste between class and practice, and, as a consequence, punctuality is actually improved. Rather than fooling around or getting into trouble before practice, players must hustle from class straight to the practice field.

Flex, Fundamentals, and Team Cal

The practice begins with a twenty-minute warm-up session. Each group spends about eight minutes doing light stretches, being careful not to overstretch and pull a muscle. Each group spends the next eight minutes on the fundamentals of that particular position. The final four minutes of this period are used for team calisthenics. This is mostly to build unity and spirit as a team. Because so much of the practice time is spent in groups, it is important to come together as a team before beginning the real practice schedule.

During the flex and fundamentals time, break up the players into the following groups:

Centers and Quarterbacks

After stretching, this group works on taking snaps. Begin by throwing easily back and forth for five minutes, ten to fifteen yards apart. This should get them sufficiently warmed up. If not, ask them to take it easy during offensive drill time until they feel ready to throw full out.

Of course, all quarterbacks must be good ball handlers, and it takes no talent to be a good faker, only self-discipline. Each day during the fundamentals period the quarterbacks work with the centers on the exchange. We use the right hand under the center and the left hand at a forty-five-degree angle with the thumbs overlapping. The center turns the football as he brings it up so the laces hit the quarterback's top hand. The quarterback automatically closes on the football with the bottom hand.

Each quarterback does the ball fakes and footwork as though the entire backfield were involved in the drill. Stress discipline in footwork at this time, going over plays in a step-by-step progression if necessary until each quarterback is comfortable with the play action.

Each day during the offensive isolation period go over the entire run offense with the quarterbacks and all the backs. Don't use any gimmicks or special drills to improve ball handling. The greatest improvement occurs through constant repetition. Each quarterback brings the football into his midsection upon receiving the snap from the center and makes handoffs and fakes from that ball position. Any time a veer action is required, make sure of a good sink into the stomach of the fullback with the football and stress dipping the front end of the ball toward the ground upon the release. This action eliminates the fullback's catching the point of the football on his hip, which generally results in a fumble.

On all running plays demand that the quarterback carry out a full-speed fake after handing off the football. A good option or bootleg fake may hold some defenders and enable the running back to have a better opportunity for a big gain.

On the option pitch ask the quarterback to settle just prior to faking the pitch, with his weight on his heels. As he pitches the football, his forward momentum should be terminated. This eases the shock of an aggressive tackle by the defensive end. The pitch is made with a flip of the wrist, turning the thumb underneath at the same time. This action produces a firm but dead ball that is easy to handle.

Diagram 2.1 shows a simple drill in which each quarterback takes snaps from each center.

COACH

Diagram 2.1   QB/Center Drill

The coach stands in front of the group and signals the play to the quarterback on the end of the line. The quarterback then calls the play and snap count. Each quarterback and center then executes the play in unison on the play caller's cadence. Run two plays and then rotate. The quarterbacks rotate left to right, and the centers stay in place. This not only is a good ball handling drill but allows each quarterback a daily review of the play signaling system.

Emphasize one fundamental per day. Don't ask the players to concentrate on all seven fundamentals at once! During practice, if the quarterback throws a poor pass, ask him what fundamental breakdown occurred. He should know the answer.

Counting warm-up, offensive isolation, goal line pass, and team offense, each of the quarterbacks throws approximately 300 passes per day. Have them throw hard (i.e., a lot) on Mondays and Wednesdays and easier on Tuesdays, which are basically play action and screen pass days. Even though Thursday is a short day, each quarterback throws nearly 1,000 passes each week.

Running Backs

After stretching, the running backs go through a series of running, agility, or blocking technique drills. Remember, the emphasis during this time is on fundamentals. It should not be used as a full-speed hit-drill period. This should be regarded as a teaching period.

> *Note:* **This time may be used to put in a new play; combine the running backs with the quarterbacks and centers and teach the new play techniques.**

Offensive Line

After stretching, the offensive linemen use this period to work on stance and footwork fundamentals. Pulling techniques and downfield blocking angles are also taught. The line coaches also use this period to review line calls (chapter 3).

Defensive Line

After stretching, the defensive linemen first use this period to work on basic alignment and stance. Second, they work on defensive techniques against the run and the pass. Also, during this time the defensive linemen may work on slanting, looping, and other stunts.

> *Note:* **This is also a good time to go over tips gained from the scouting reports or films of the upcoming opponent.**

Defensive Backs

After stretching, the defensive backs work on footwork drills and reacting to the ball. Also, they work on some zone or man-to-man coverage drills.

Split Ends

After stretching, the split ends work on pass receiving drills. The one-hand catch, the great effort, and the sideline catch drills are used most frequently. Try to get as many repetitions as possible by using at least two throwers. If needed, release one of the quarterbacks to work with the split ends during this time period. It is important not to have receivers standing around at any time (Diagrams 2.2 to 2.4).

One-Hand Catch. This is a good warm-up drill that helps develop "soft" hands and hand-eye coordination. Have the receivers form two lines, facing each other, and run up routes, looking over their inside shoulders. Make sure they catch the pass with the outside hand and give with the ball. The hand should be loose and relaxed. Emphasize that they should try to catch with the hand and *not* the body. Rotate to the opposite line and give the football to quarterback.

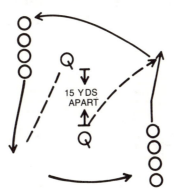

Diagram 2.2   Warm-Up Alignment

Great Effort. Using the same lines, have the receivers run up routes. The quarterback should throw the pass over the outside shoulder. Teach the receivers to turn the head as quickly as possible to the outside, relocate the ball, run it down, and snatch it out of the air.

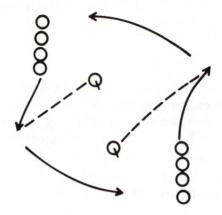

Diagram 2.3   Warm-Up Alignment Continued

> *Note:* **In both of the above drills (Diagrams 2.2 and 2.3) the ball should be run back to the quarterback (or coach) and the receiver should then switch lines.**

Sideline Catch.   Move the line to the hash mark, facing the sideline. On the quarterback's signal the receiver breaks to the sideline, focusing on a spot between the quarterback and the route angle. Out of his peripheral vision he will be able to locate both the football and the sideline. Return the ball to the same line.

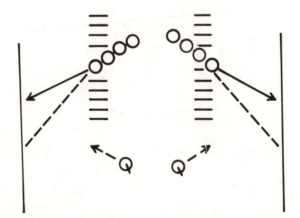

Diagram 2.4   Sideline Catch

Kicking Game

The next twenty-minute block of time is reserved for the kicking game. It is impossible to cover the entire kicking game during this time, so spend ten minutes each on Point After Touchdown (PAT) and field goals (Diagram 2.5). Cover this phase of the kicking game every day. For PAT and field goal practice, run two groups. Each group runs three plays at a time before returning to the huddle. The defense stays the same and tries to give different looks in attempting to block the kick.

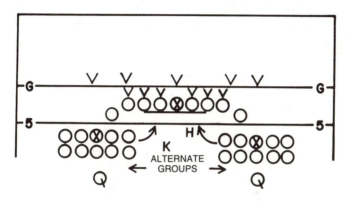

Diagram 2.5   PAT Drill

Note: **Practice any fake kicks at this time.**

Practice punt coverage as part of the conditioning period and punt return during the last five minutes of kicking time on Tuesday and Thursday (Diagram 2.6).

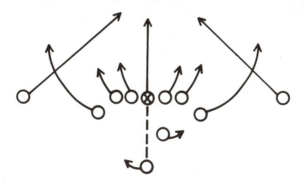

Diagram 2.6   Punt Formation

Note: **All kickers should work out during the fundamentals period each day.**

Because of the punt alignment, the defense is forced to cover all four receivers. With at least one player for returning the punt, that leaves six to rush the punter, and six offensive blockers. If the defense leaves one of the receivers uncovered, automatic to a bingo route (chapter 4), snap the ball to the quarterback, and throw the pass.

Each coach must evaluate his own priorities for spending time practicing the kicking game. We spend most of our kicking time on blocking for the punt and relatively little time on the return, even though our punt return people spend all of their warm-up time fielding punts.

Thursday is a review day for the entire kicking game, and on this day we spend whatever time is necessary to work out any problems.

Defensive Isolation

During the next half-hour, divide the players into four groups for defensive isolation. Use two groups if half-line drills are run.

During isolation the sophomore, junior, and senior players work together and spend all of the time with drills concerning each individual position. Sometimes groups are combined; for example, the defensive backs and the linebackers may be together on pass defense. Or, the linebackers, defensive ends, and linemen work together as a front against the run. Of course, it is sometimes necessary to have a group of offensive players servicing the defense. Assign a coach to be in charge of that group, and supply him with play cards if necessary.

During the half-line, it is necessary to have two offensive half-line groups. However, because there are only two groups on defense, numbers should never be a problem (Diagram 2.7).

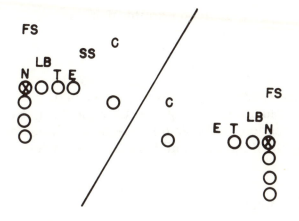

Diagram 2.7   Half-Line Alignment

Note: **It is necessary to have two nose guards and two free safeties. Alternate them between groups so they can work against both the strong and the weak sides.**

Team Defense

Start the team defense on the goal line. This emphasizes the importance of the goal line defense. Try to get at least five minutes per day on the goal line. Doing four live plays from the three-yard line has a way of bringing out great enthusiasm. Be careful not to do full-speed plays too often because of possible injuries! Also, have a very quick whistle during this drill.

Fifteen minutes of open-field team defense may not seem like a lot, but it is enough to tie the parts together and leave the defense hungry and not overtrained. In fact, the defensive coaches will skip team defense entirely on some days in order to spend more time on isolation or half-line, which they feel may be more beneficial to go over on those occasions.

Offensive Isolation

This is a daily thirty-minute period. The linemen always work by themselves. The backs and ends usually spend fifteen minutes alone and fifteen minutes working together on some aspect of the passing game.

Offensive Line

The time is usually split between the blocking sled, run blocking, pass blocking, and special play blocking. Spend some time, as needed, on basic one-on-one blocking. In addition, each day the linemen should spend time on defensive recognition.

Offensive Backs

Each day the backs go over the entire run offense. Usually two groups work back to back, alternating snaps so the coaches can watch both groups. If numbers are smaller, one group will suffice (Diagram 2.8).

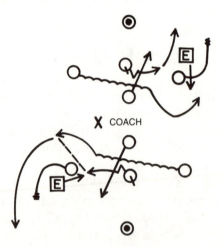

Diagram 2.8   Backfield Drill Alignment

> *Note:* **Place a cone at least twenty yards upfield. The ball carrier must sprint past the cone on each play!**

Timing is very important, so strive to get in as many repetitions as possible. Run each of the running plays first to the right and then to the left. Also, try to keep the starters working together, the seconds together, and so on, to maintain proper continuity.

During the second fifteen minutes of offensive isolation, have the backs and ends work together on some phase of the pass offense.

Split Ends

The first five minutes is always spent on form blocking, using the stalk-blocking technique. We ask the receiver to break down when the defensive back reacts to the run, and screen him by moving the feet to stay in front of him and reacting to his first movement. He should not throw at the defensive back or initiate the block, but be more like a counter-puncher. The crack-back block is used about ten percent of the time; the players should be very careful to block above the waist! For the next ten minutes work on individual routes (chapter 5), always throwing to each receiver. If not enough coaches are available to throw, supply them with quarterbacks from the run offense drills.

Next, combine the backs and ends, and run a pass skeleton drill (Diagram 2.9).

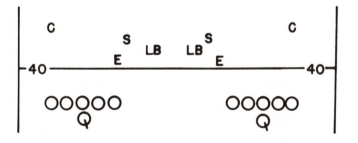

Diagram 2.9   Pass Skeleton Alignment

> *Note:* **Always throw on a marked field. Start on the forty-yard line and move the ball on each completion. This will provide good experience for game situations.**

Try to cover all the basic patterns and any new or special patterns at this time. Run one defensive group (with alternates) and two offensive groups (with alternates). Sometimes the younger players should watch, and sometimes they should break off on their own.

Team Offense

Team offense usually lasts for thirty minutes, but take extra time if necessary. It is important to let the players know if extra time will be needed in practice. This helps not only to motivate but also to keep them from being surprised if practice goes longer than usual.

During team offense try to put the best players on defense who are not alternating on offense. Rarely, if ever, is this time used for scrimmage. Instead, go full speed to the ball defensively with *no* tackling. This is called *thuds.* Do not allow the offensive blockers to cut-block, and always warn the defensive player of a crack block. Thuds provides a good simulation without risking injury.

> *Note:* **Blocking dummies are not required, but arm shields are handy and seem to work much better.**

Begin on the forty-yard line and move the ball on each play. Mix up the defenses, working against the standard defenses. In addition, work against any special defense that you may have seen in the past from the opponent.

Each day spend about fifteen minutes during the team session working on special formations—usually a different set Monday through Wednesday. On Thursday, go over only those plays that will be used that particular week.

> *Note:* **Use a cone line to keep room around the offensive huddle. Players must keep behind this line at all times. It will help tremendously in keeping order in and around the huddle.**

Try to work at least five minutes per day with a group made up of the younger players who will play when the game is out of reach in the fourth quarter. Give them a few simple plays, not the entire offense. This ensures that they have an opportunity to be successful and, more importantly, that they know the plays. Too often young players get discouraged or injured late in a runaway game because someone runs the wrong way or misses an assignment.

Conditioning

Spend the last ten to fifteen minutes of each practice on conditioning. Change the conditioning drill each day, and do no conditioning on Thursday. You can also add a group cooldown stretch at the end of the conditioning period.

Summary

The practices are lengthy, but organized. Kids don't mind long practices if they are organized and if they can see the purpose of each period. By keeping the contact to a minimum, seldom will a boy be injured in practice, and the players are always eager for Friday night's contact.

At the midseason point we cut practice time in half; each individual session is reduced by half. We spend almost no time on fundamentals and nearly all the time on game preparation. If it looks like the fundamentals are becoming sloppy, we spend an entire practice period on the fundamentals, usually a Monday. This change of pace is mentally uplifting and has worked well for us. Of course, it is possible to cut practice time in any session to fit the individual circumstances of your school.

Chapter

3

Run and Pass Blocking

It makes no difference what type of offense you believe in or attempt to run. If you don't prepare your offensive line, it will have little or no chance for success. Try to help the linemen out by teaching them proper technique and giving them simple rules with built-in flexibility. This chapter begins with number blocking rules and follows with line calls and pass blocking rules. All of the blocking schemes and rules for the double slot offense are covered here. The pass rules are broken into basic frontside and backside rules that cover all possible stunts and are easy to learn.

Number Blocking

As in most blocking schemes it is necessary to number the defense. This numbering system is very basic. The defensive man over the center is 0, the next man is Number 1, and so forth (Diagram 3.1). The center blocks 0 in man blocking; the guard blocks Number 1, and the tackle Number 2. The slot-back or the fullback blocks Number 3 except on option plays.

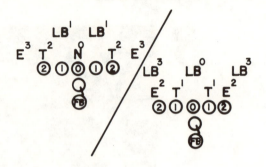

Diagram 3.1   Defensive Numbering

The split and stack defenses are two defensive schemes or adjustments that we see often. Because both defenses do not fit the regular numbering system it is necessary to cover them separately. The split defense follows the number rule with one minor exception. Because there is no player directly over the center, 0 becomes the first player on the backside (away from the play direction). The center always steps to the onside guard center gap before blocking 0. The guard and tackle to the frontside will combo-block Numbers 1 and 2 (Diagram 3.2).

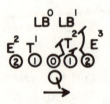

Diagram 3.2   Numbering Vs. Split Defense

If you are up against a stack defense, it is necessary to zone block the area of the stack, always protecting the inside gap first (Diagram 3.3).

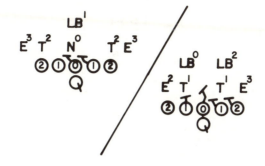

Diagram 3.3 Numbering Vs. Stack Defense

Line Calls

The center identifies the defense and makes a call at the line of scrimmage. He calls "50" for the 5-2, "40" for the 4-3 or 6-1 (they look the same to the offense), "split" for the split 4 or split 6, "stack" for any of the stack defenses, and "gap" for any gap-type defense. These calls help the offensive tackle make a proper line call for the blocking scheme. Communication between the offensive linemen is vital, making it possible to eliminate the busted play.

The tackles usually make the line calls but at times the guards make the calls. There are eleven possible line calls. Try to take advantage of blocking angles in determining which blocking scheme to call. During the fundamentals period go over defensive alignments and determine the best line calls for certain plays. Impress upon the linemen that they should use the line calls to their own advantage in blocking the defense. The tackles make a call on every play but the call is only live on plays to their side.

1. **Man:**

   Block man-on-man using the numbering system.

2. **Combo:**

   Refers to a combination block between the guard and tackle; most often used against the split defense (Diagram 3.4).

Diagram 3.4   Combo Technique

3. **Down:**
   Block the first man inside; used against gap defenses, and trap and veer blocking (Diagram 3.5).

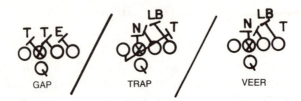

Diagram 3.5   Down Technique

4. **Swing:**
   The guard pulls and seal-blocks a linebacker inside; most often used against the "50" defense (Diagram 3.6).

Diagram 3.6   Swing Technique

5. **You:**
   A cross-block between the guard and tackle in which the guard goes first; most often used against the "50" defense (Diagram 3.7).

Diagram 3.7 You (Cross) Technique

6. **I:**

A cross-block between the guard and tackle in which the tackle goes first; most often used against the "40" defense (Diagram 3.8).

Diagram 3.8 I (Cross) Technique

7. **Check:**

The guard makes this call, which refers to a cross-block (or fill block) between the center and backside guard; used against the "40" defense (Diagram 3.9).

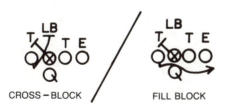

CROSS – BLOCK / FILL BLOCK

Diagram 3.9 Check Technique

8. **Reach:**

Another guard call that refers to filling for the frontside guard against the "40" defense (Diagram 3.10).

Diagram 3.10   Reach Technique

9. **Base:**

This is a tackle call that refers to a combo-block with the slotback; used on counter and buck sweep (Diagram 3.11).

Diagram 3.11   Basic Technique

10. **Sucker:**

Used by the guard or tackle to show pass and influence the defensive linemen across the line of scrimmage to be trapped; usually called on draw trap (Diagram 3.12).

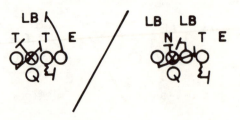

Diagram 3.12   Sucker Technique

11. **Zone:**

Used when facing a stack defense that is stunting a lot. Refers to blocking the first man to enter the inside gap zone (Diagram 3.13).

Diagram 3.13 Zone Technique

Pass Rules

Frontside rules refer to the side the ball is on; therefore, front-side can be either right or left depending on the direction of the play as called in the huddle.

Frontside 1, Inside Gap
Anytime the inside gap is challenged the lineman must take a parallel step with the inside foot and protect the gap (Diagram 3.14).

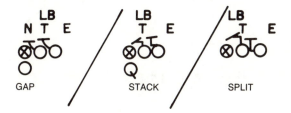

Diagram 3.14 Inside Gap Technique

> *Note:* **The inside gap rule takes precedence over all other rules.**

Frontside 2, Head Up
If the inside gap is not challenged, block anyone head up, on or off the line of scrimmage (this means any down lineman or linebacker rushing the passer).

Frontside 3, Backside
If the inside gap is not challenged and the lineman is covered by a linebacker who does not rush the passer, then he loses

ground straight backward, turns toward the backside, and blocks the first backside rush.

> *Note:* **The center is considered a frontside pass blocker. Therefore, on a pass to the right his first responsibility is the gap between himself and the left guard.**

Backside 1, Head Up

The backside guard and tackle need not protect their inside gap because it will be blocked by the center or onside guard (Diagram 3.15). The backside guard and tackle block any player lined up, on or off the line of scrimmage, rushing the passer.

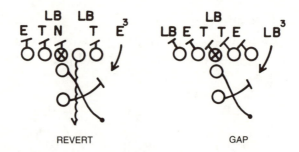

Diagram 3.15   Backside Blocking

Backside 2, Backside

If the backside guard or tackle is covered by either a linebacker who does not rush or no player at all, he loses ground and blocks the first player coming from the backside.

> *Note:* **It is vital that the offensive lineman, when blocking backside, gain depth straight back and let the pass rusher come to him.**

Common Defensive Schemes

Diagrams 3.16 to 3.18 show pass blocking against the three defenses most often used by teams defending the double slot.

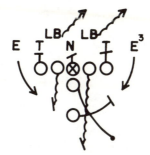

Diagram 3.16 "50" Rush Vs. "50" Defense

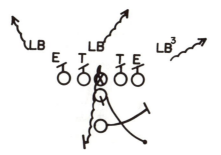

Diagram 3.17 Regular "40" Vs. "40" Defense

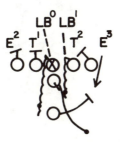

Diagram 3.18 Split Adjustments Vs. "Split 4" Defense

Note: **The split defense requires a small adjustment in pass-blocking rules. The fullback blocks the end man on the Line of Scrimmage (LOS) (3). The frontside tackle and guard combo-block 1 and 2. The backside linebacker becomes 0 and the center blocks him (Diagram 3.18).**

Stunts

Teams generally do not stunt much because of the fear of getting burned for a quick touchdown. Teams use most often a four- or five-man rush, sometimes a six-man rush, and almost never a seven-man rush. Eight-man rushes come under the heading of safety blitzes and are covered in chapter 9. There are many stunts that defenses can use to put a good pass rush on the quarterback. It would be impossible to diagram all stunts; however, the following stunts are seen most often (Diagrams 3.19 to 3.27).

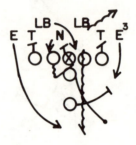

Diagram 3.19   Scrape Stunt

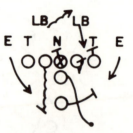

Diagram 3.20   Frontside Blitz

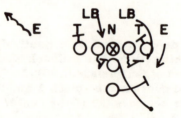

Diagram 3.21   Two-Linebacker Stunt

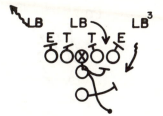

Diagram 3.22   Scrape Stunt

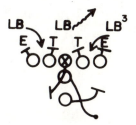

Diagram 3.23   X Stunt

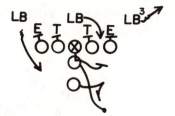

Diagram 3.24   Frontside Drop

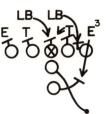

Diagram 3.25   Scrape

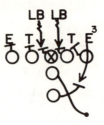

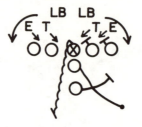

Diagram 3.26 Blow

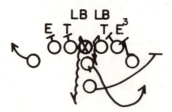

Diagram 3.27 Loop

If an extra blocker is needed, call "1–18" or "1–19"; the "1" tells the frontside slotback to remain in as a blocker. This is occasionally done against a split defense to help the quarterback get outside the pass rush (Diagram 3.28).

Diagram 3.28 Sprint Out

The double slot blocking scheme requires the offensive linemen to think and talk. This system has stood the test of time and has served the offense well. Tell the linemen, "When in doubt, point at the man you are blocking," so there is no confusion on the line of scrimmage. Having the linemen make calls at the line of scrimmage not only challenges them but makes them feel more a part of the offense.

The Fullback Block

On pass plays the fullback always blocks the frontside number 3 (Diagram 3.1). If the defensive end rushes to the outside (Diagram 3.29), the fullback blocks him at an inside-out angle, using a surface block, with his inside shoulder. He should attack with enough force to keep from being driven back into the quarterback, but at the same time not overextending. If the defensive end is blitzing hard (Diagram 3.30), the fullback uses a crossbody block with his head toward the outside. This collision usually knocks down the defensive end and enables the quarterback to get outside the pass rush and either run or pass. If the defensive end drops off into pass coverage, the fullback blocks the first defender to show (Diagram 3.31).

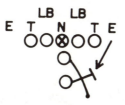

Diagram 3.29   Surface Block

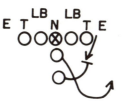

Diagram 3.30   Crossbody Block

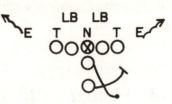

Diagram 3.31   Help Block

The Seven-Man Rush

Because of the short passing game and the fear of the big play, a seven-man pass rush is not seen very often. If facing a team that consistently uses the seven-man rush, however, use the passing attack, opposite motion. By sprinting away from motion and using the motion back in the blocking scheme, all seven pass rushers can be blocked (Diagram 3.32).

If the defense is rushing seven players, they must play man to man in the secondary in order to cover all the receivers. A favorite pattern against the seven-man rush is a scramble route by the frontside split end, combined with a throwback switch pattern with the two backside receivers. A sting of the basic pattern is also excellent against the seven-man rush (see "Sting," chapter 5).

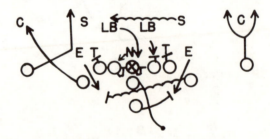

Diagram 3.32   Seven-Man Rush

Chapter
4

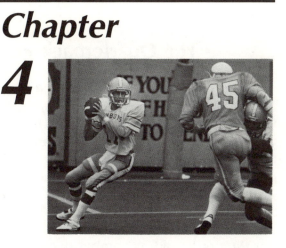

Quarterback, the Trigger Man

This chapter will help you to determine not only who your quarterback will be but also how to improve his passing ability. Specifically, this chapter answers the following questions: What are the attributes that a winning quarterback must have? What type athlete must he be? What kind of arm must he have?

All coaches have had quarterbacks with varying levels of ability and totally different personalities. Some of our own quarterbacks have had great talent, whereas some have had average ability. Some have had success related to their outstanding individual talent, whereas others were able to gain all-star recognition mainly because of this particular offense.

The Quarterback Personality

Regardless of his basic personality, the quarterback must have some characteristic that commands the respect of his teammates. This respect is vital to his success as an individual and ultimately to your success as a team.

He need not be a superstar nor a valedictorian; however, he must possess that one characteristic that his teammates will respect. All of our quarterbacks have had one common trait: the willingness to work hard. In addition, some of them have been respected for their awesome physical abilities, some for their outstanding competitiveness, some for their coolness under fire, some for their leadership abilities, and some for their ability to get the job done. Your quarterback need not be the one with the best arm—accuracy is much more important. Finally he must be the one player that the team will perform for on game day!

Physical Attributes

Every coach would like his quarterback to be tall, fast, and talented. Because this is not always possible, it is up to you to determine the abilities of your chosen quarterback and adjust the offense to his capabilities. Allow him to be successful by building your offense around his strengths. Don't under any circumstances ask him to do something he is not physically able to do! He need not be your best athlete, although that would help. If he is not a naturally gifted passer, he must be willing to practice until he is better than average. You can make a boy with reasonable athletic ability into a better-than-average passer. Quarterback is a unique position and, in a wide-open offense, vital to your success. However, he doesn't have to be of all-state caliber physically; look for someone who is hard working and willing to learn. When in doubt, take your six-foot-two basketball guard (he can run, has good hand-eye coordination, can think on the move) and give him a quarterback number; you probably won't go wrong!

Throwing Checklist

A word about the grip: Because each boy's hands are of different size, there is no perfect way to grip the football. Simply have him hold onto the ball where it feels most comfortable to him. Be sure that he grips the ball with his fingers and not his palm.

The throwing motion is a coordinated action that involves the entire body. You don't throw with just your arm. Throwing a football (specifically the action in the legs, hips, and shoulders) is similar to pitching a baseball, hitting a golf ball, or swinging a tennis racket.

Follow the seven points listed below when teaching your quarterback how to throw the football. Make a videotape of the seven points if you can; it is a great teaching tool that enables you to make sure the fundamentals are correct. The old saying, "A picture is worth a thousand words," was never more applicable.

1. Firm wrist

The wrist should be firm throughout the entire motion. Do not allow the wrist to turn by itself as a separate part of the throwing motion. Rather, let it move naturally as the shoulder rotates backward and forward. If the wrist is too loose, the point of the ball will be inconsistent with the release and the result will be a ball that wobbles. If your quarterback is throwing a wobbly ball, a loose wrist is probably the cause. Tell him to firm up the wrist and the proper spiral should return.

2. Coordinate shoulder turn

Passing the football requires that you throw while moving both shoulders together. Point the lead shoulder at the target. It will move in unison with the forward movement of the throwing shoulder on a horizontal plane. The most common error is to pull out too soon with the lead shoulder, which leaves the throwing shoulder to perform by itself. The result is a lack of velocity and usually a lack of consistent accuracy.

If your quarterback lacks velocity, it is probably the result of poor shoulder-turn fundamentals. Check to be sure his lead shoulder is not releasing too soon. Greater velocity and greater range will be the result. Also, the ball may be delivered too high if lead shoulder problems exist.

3. Elbows at shoulder level

Both elbows should be at shoulder level prior to the forward motion. The weight is evenly distributed at the start of the delivery, and, as the throwing motion begins, the weight transfers to the front foot. The throwing elbow remains above shoulder level during the throwing motion prior to the release of the ball. Strive for a three-quarter motion. The lead elbow should be bent with the fist held close to the body. This fairly tight position of the lead arm and hand will help control the shoulder turn and help eliminate any early release of the lead shoulder and all its resulting problems.

4. Straight arm follow-through

To insure a proper follow-through the throwing hand should end up somewhere between the opposite groin and the outside of the opposite thigh. The arm should be straight and the elbow locked. If your quarterback is throwing the ball too high, it is probably due in part to poor follow-through. He should help the problem by making a complete straight arm follow-through.

5. Head over front foot

This concerns the proper weight transfer that is so important for the quarterback. The best way to check this is to see if the head is directly over the front foot after the release of the ball. The front knee will be locked, and all the weight will be transferred to the front leg. If your quarterback has trouble throwing the ball too low, check for an overstride. To reduce overstriding, make sure his feet are close together on the set-up. Proper stride should help eliminate this problem.

6. Air under back heel

Another way to check for proper weight transfer is to watch the back heel. As the weight transfers to the front foot during the throwing motion, the back heel should lift off the ground. At the finish of the throw, the toe should be pointed to the ground. Most good passers finish with the back foot completely off the ground.

7. Head still and vertical

No matter how hard you throw the football or how long the pass is, the head should remain as still as possible during the motion. It should not move off the vertical plane. This is a good guide for the shoulder turn. If the head moves off the vertical plane, the lead shoulder has left too soon, pulling the head with it.

A good exercise to improve head position is to place a piece of tape at shoulder level, horizontally on a mirror; intersect that with a vertical piece of tape. Now position yourself in front of the mirror and go through the throwing motion, checking to make sure your head stays on the vertical plane and your shoulders stay on the horizontal plane.

The Quarterback Drops

Three types of quarterback drops are used in the double slot offense: the two-step, the three-step, and the five-step drop. The two-step drop is a straight-back drop, whereas the three- and five-step drops are at a forty-five-degree angle from the line of scrimmage. The two-step drop is used for all quick slant routes and for all hot and double-up patterns. The three-step drop is used for the first option on the sting pattern and all flood and x patterns. The five-step drop is used on all other routes and patterns.

It is very important that all quarterbacks have good footwork, which makes the job of accurately throwing the football much easier.

Note: **For the sake of simplicity footwork diagrams show right-handed quarterbacks only.**

Two-Step Drop

The footwork is slightly different depending on the direction of the throw. The quarterback should start with his feet parallel, approximately twelve inches apart. The right-handed quarterback always starts the two-step drop with the left foot first. With two normal steps he should be 2 1/2 to 3 yards off the line of scrimmage.

On the throw to the right it is necessary to toe-out the right foot, toward the receiver, *before* setting the foot down (Diagram 4.1). This makes it possible for the quarterback to take his short, third step with the lead foot directly at the receiver, without shuffling the feet. For a pass to the left it is necessary to toe-in the right foot *before* setting the foot down (Diagram 4.2).

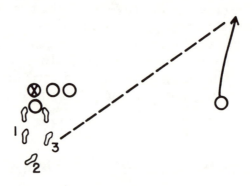

Diagram 4.1   Two-Step Drop for a Right Pass (Right-Handed QB)

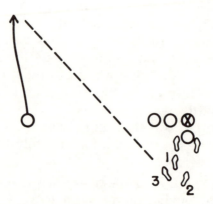

Diagram 4.2   Two-Step Drop for a Left Pass (Right-Handed QB)

The Drop Right (three- or five-step)

For directional drops, right or left, begin with the foot to the direction side (open step, do not reverse pivot). For both the drop to the right (Diagram 4.3) and the throwback (Diagram 4.4), the quarterback throws off the third (or fifth) step while taking a short direction step with the front foot. For the three-step drop, the quarterback throws from a five-yard depth, directly behind the offensive guard. For the five-step drop, he throws from an eight- to ten-yard depth, directly behind the offensive tackle. The three-step drop is shown to the right and the five-step drop to the left.

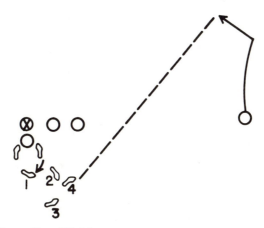

Diagram 4.3   Three-Step Right

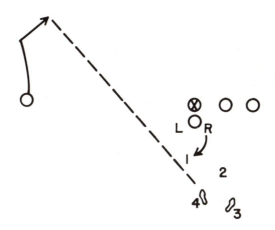

Diagram 4.4   Three-Step Right, Throwback

For the throwback the quarterback must toe-in the right foot *before* setting it down, just as in the two-step drop. This makes the short direction step easy to do without having to shuffle the feet (Diagram 4.4).

The Drop Left (three- or five-step)

On the drop to the left, for a right-handed quarterback, it is necessary to pivot on the toe on the third or fifth step and plant the right foot the fourth or sixth step. Therefore, it takes one more step to set up going to the left (Diagram 4.5). For the sake of consistency, all drops are called three- or five-step drops. This also makes it less confusing for the quarterback. It is important to make sure that the quarterback keeps his feet close together when he makes his pivot; this keeps him from overstriding.

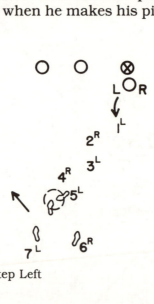

Diagram 4.5   Five-Step Left

On the throwback from the drop left, it becomes necessary to make an even greater pivot on the last step to get in proper position for the throw (Diagram 4.6).

Even though the right-handed quarterback takes an extra step going to the left, the timing of the throw has not been affected.

It may seem unimportant to spend a lot of time on quarterback footwork. However, by stressing proper footwork fundamentals the quarterbacks will be able to set up quicker and therefore have more time to read the receiver and deliver the

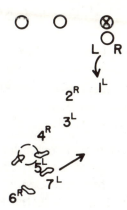

Diagram 4.6   Five-Step Left, Throwback

ball on target. The extra time it takes to learn the proper foot-work will be time well spent, and your offense will reap the benefits.

The Quarterback Challenge

Like most things in football, what is asked of the quarterback is not unique to any one program. Most of the quarterback philosophy taught has been learned from talking with other coaches, attending clinics, and reading books.

Quarterback is a unique position in football. No other position demands such a burden of responsibility, and no other player demands such desire to excel, or such respect by his teammates. What is demanded of him off the field may be as important as what is demanded of him on it. Not everybody can accept the challenge of playing quarterback. In many ways he must be a special individual. Look for the following traits in the quarterback candidate:

Character—He must be above reproach both on and off the field.

Attitude—He must be able to present a positive attitude to the football team and generate within the team an objective to win.

Desire—He must be willing to work many hours to improve skills.

Respect—Teammates must respect his human decency and look to him in moments of pressure.

Ability—He must have above-average ability in quarterback skills, and, more importantly, he must be able to display those skills on game day.

The natural ability of a quarterback candidate is often times less important than the other requirements, but the more physical skills an athlete possesses, the better chance he has of becoming the starting quarterback.

Leadership is a responsibility that can be learned. The quarterback who is a positive influence on his teammates will be a winner. Leadership traits can be defined as those qualities that are of greatest assistance in obtaining confidence, respect, and loyal cooperation from one's teammates:

Integrity—Uprightness of character, soundness of moral principles, and absolute truthfulness.

Knowledge—Well-versed in the game of football and understanding of his teammates.

Courage—A mental quality that recognizes fear, danger, or criticism, but enables that player to proceed in the face of it with calmness and firmness.

Decisiveness—The ability to reach decisions promptly and to announce them in a clear, forceful manner.

Dependability—Dependability and reliability in terms of performance of his tasks.

Initiative—The ability to see what has to be done and do it even in the absence of supervision of a coach.

Tact—The ability to deal with others without creating offense or petty jealousy.

Enthusiasm—The display of sincere interest and exuberance in the game. He must be one of those players who *loves* to play.

Resilience—The ability to bounce back from setbacks and accept constructive criticism.

Unselfishness—The ability to place the team above his personal advancement, giving others credit at all times.

Loyalty—Faithfulness to the coaching staff, the school, and the team.

The following are leadership principles that, if followed, will give the quarterback candidate the opportunity to become a leader:

1. Be technically and tactically proficient.
2. Know yourself and seek self-improvement.
3. Know your teammates and look out for their welfare.
4. Set a *positive* example.
5. Seek responsibility and take responsibility for your own actions.

Summary

Above all, the quarterback candidate must develop a strong self-concept. A good leader has to be in command of his own emotions before he can command his teammates. The ideal quarterback is a tall, talented, and intelligent athlete, but you won't find many who fit this ideal. Instead, take that kid who is willing to work hard, has the respect of his teammates, and is a reasonably good athlete, and make him your quarterback. Teach him the proper throwing motion, continually using the seven points listed, and let him throw a thousand times a week. He will become very proficient, and you will be on your way to an exciting and successful season.

Chapter

5

Receiver Routes and Sting, the Basic Pattern

This chapter covers the routes used by the split ends and slot-backs, as well as specific detail on the scramble route and the sting pattern.

All of football's basic routes are used in the double slot passing scheme. The only difference is that descriptive names or phrases are used to describe routes or patterns, whereas most schemes use numbers. At times a particular route will be called to either a split end or a slotback; however, most of the time the routes are used within a pattern, also described by name (chapters 6, 7, and 8).

> *Note:* **A route refers to an individual route whereas a pattern is a combination of routes.**

The individual routes are taught during the fundamentals period at the beginning of each practice. They are then reviewed during this period for the remainder of the season. To keep interest at a high level, use competitive drills during this period between the right- and left-side receivers.

> *Note:* **Spend most of the offensive isolation time on patterns rather than on individual routes.**

Five to ten minutes per day is spent on stalk blocking, and the rest of the time the receivers catch the football as many times as possible. Nothing improves a receiver more than repetition. In the normal practice day each receiver should catch somewhere from 80 to 100 passes. With that many opportunities, it will not take the players long to develop individual receiving skills. Some very average players have become all-stars through hard work and repetition. Give your kids a chance to be successful through repetition, and it won't be long before they are making great catches on game day.

Split End Routes

These are the routes to be run and practiced during the fundamentals period with either quarterbacks or coaches throwing (Diagram 5.1).

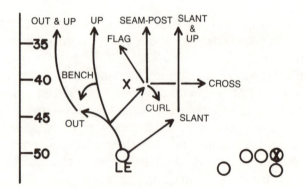

Diagram 5.1   Split End Passing Tree

Slotback Routes

The slotback pass routes will be practiced daily during the fundamentals period. Begin by running at one-half to three-quarter speed before progressing to full speed as expertise dictates (Diagram 5.2).

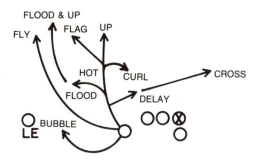

Diagram 5.2   Slotback Passing Tree

> *Note:* **The slotback can run all the same routes after motion (see Diagram 5.3).**

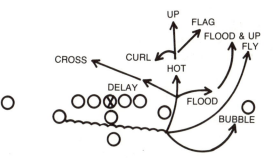

Diagram 5.3   Passing Tree From Motion

The Scramble Route

In the scramble route, the receiver can run any route he wants. The receiver must have a clock in his head and make his final break at the count of four. By working with the quarterbacks it is not long before the timing becomes second nature for the receiver.

Use scramble a lot against a man-to-man defense. It enables the receiver to use his natural ability and instincts to get himself open. It is surprising how easy it is for the quarterback to read the scramble route and deliver the ball on target.

Note: **It is important for the other three receivers to keep clear of the area of the scramble (Diagram 5.4).**

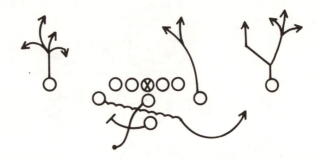

Diagram 5.4   Split End Scramble: "19 Roar, LE Scramble"

If a pattern for the remaining three receivers is not called, they are free to run any route.

Many times on a split end scramble a backside pattern will be called and the motion back will block the backside defensive end for maximum protection (Diagram 5.5).

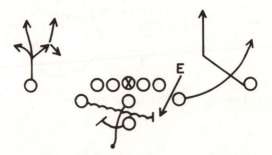

Diagram 5.5 Scramble With Maximum Protection: "19 Rip, LE Scramble-Throwback Switch"

Scramble can be run with the slotback as well. It can be run with no motion (Diagram 5.6) or with motion (Diagram 5.7). The quarterback action can be either toward or away from the receiver.

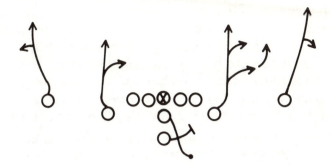

Diagram 5.6   Slot Scramble: "18 Right, Half Scramble"

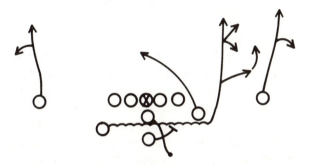

Diagram 5.7   Slot Scramble With Motion: "18 Rip, LH Scramble"

On slotback scramble tell the split ends to run up or out routes and the opposite slot to stay out of the middle of the field. Of course, you can add a throwback pattern to slotback scramble (Diagram 5.8).

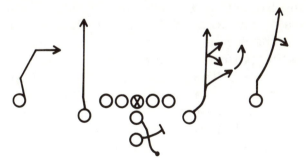

Diagram 5.8   Scramble Combination: "18 RH Scramble, Throwback Touchdown"

The scramble route fits in well with the wide-open style of play. It also seems to give the receivers a certain freedom that they relish. They are free to try new tricks and new routes that they may have picked up by watching other receivers or their favorite pro player. Although this route dates back to the days of the sandlots when football was simple and the quarterback would say, "You get open and I'll throw you the ball," it is by no means a sandlot play in terms of effectiveness.

Note: **A good time to work on the scramble is during the one-on-one period with the defensive backs.**

Sting's Six Options

Most coaches have a base play around which they build their offense—one play by which they can be identified. For example, USC has the "student body right," Oklahoma the "triple option," and Houston the "veer." These plays have been refined over the years and each has become the play to be stopped when defensing the particular team. In the double slot offense the base play has become what, in our terminology, is called *sting.* What started out as a relatively simple quick pass away from motion has been refined into the play that all defenses must stop first.

The beauty of motion from a balanced formation like the double slot is that it will create an offensive overload. Therefore, the defense must also overload their secondary in some manner to be defensively sound. What this usually creates is a one-on-one situation between the split end away from motion and the defensive back on that side. In effect, the play dictates a man-to-man defense at that spot regardless of whether the actual defense is man or zone.

The sting pattern is a four-receiver pattern that involves a two-part route by the onside split end, a read option route by the stationary slot, a deep threat by the backside split end, and a delay by the motion slot (Diagram 5.9). Combine these routes with a simple decision-making process by the quarterback, and it becomes a play around which you can build an offense.

Built into the pattern are six routes. By running the sting to both sides, twelve pass plays, in effect, have been created

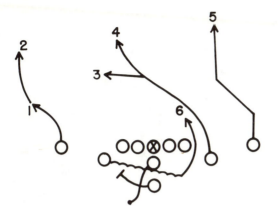

Diagram 5.9   The Full Pattern: "19 Rip, Sting"

out of one pattern. The question is often asked, "How is it possible to teach so many plays?" Part of the answer is by designing plays such as sting that have six plays built into one pattern. What looks very complex is actually very simple.

The Speed Cut (Option 1)

To run the sting route effectively the play-side split end must align himself with enough area into the sideline to make a good cut and still have room to make the catch and keep his feet inbounds.

Lance Alworth of the San Diego Chargers is credited with developing the speed cut. Prior to that time a receiver would always plant the inside foot for an outside cut and the outside foot for an inside cut. The problem with that method was that the receiver had to slow down to make a sharp cut. The speed cut allows the receiver to make the same sharp cut without slowing down (Diagram 5.10).

As the name implies, the speed cut is made at nearly full speed. By angling the fourth step toward the sideline and running around that foot for the fifth step, the receiver is, by the seventh step, heading into the sideline at nearly full speed. This is usually a five- to seven-yard route, depending on the length of the receiver's stride. As you can see by the darkened steps in Diagram 5.10, the receiver is almost two strides farther into the route by the seventh step when using the speed

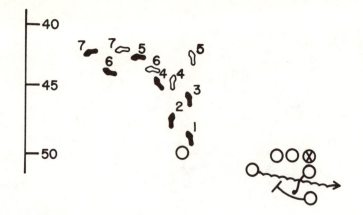

Diagram 5.10   Speed Cut Footwork

cut; the receiver gets to the seventh step a full second faster. This ability to cover more ground in less time has made the speed cut a vital part of the double slot pass offense. First walk the receivers through the steps and build up to full speed. In no time at all the players will be running excellent speed cuts.

The Out and Up (Option 2)

If the split end is open on the out cut, the ball should be in the air when the receiver first looks back to the quarterback. This makes it almost impossible to defend. If the ball has not been thrown when the receiver first looks back at the quarterback (i.e., because the defensive back is too close), the receiver immediately begins a speed cut up the sideline. He should angle the seventh step upfield and run around that foot with the eighth step. By the eleventh step the receiver should be sprinting up the sideline, looking for the ball over his inside shoulder. If the defensive back has overplayed the out part of the route, chances are good that the receiver will beat him on the up by using the speed cut. In Diagram 5.11 the darkened steps indicate where the receiver is wider and deeper when using the speed cut.

The constant threat of the out and up generally forces the defensive back to play soft on the out cut, resulting in an almost automatic six- to eight-yard gain on sting's first option.

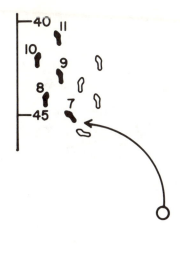

Diagram 5.11 Option Two Footwork

By using the speed cut the receivers have, in effect, become faster. In terms of distance the routes have been stretched and deepened. This forces the defensive backs to cover more ground in less time. The effect of the speed cut alone has made a tremendous difference in the success of the double slot pass offense.

The Slot Read (Options 3 and 4)

The stationary slot aligns himself in position to release either inside or outside of the defensive end (approximately a four-yard split from the offensive tackle). On the snap he runs under control, at about three-quarter speed, at a depth of six to eight yards across the secondary, keying the opposite safety.

If the slot key reacts backward, at any angle, he continues across the field at no more depth than ten yards (Diagram 5.12).

If the slot key reacts forward, he turns upfield, usually near the hash mark, and runs up the seam of the defense looking for the ball over his inside shoulder (Diagram 5.13).

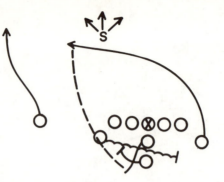

Diagram 5.12   Slot, Option Three

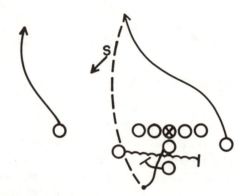

Diagram 5.13   Slot, Option Four

The Throwback Seam-Post (Option 5)

The throwback part of the sting pattern can be a real game breaker. If the defensive safeties are active and move with the quarterback action, the seam-post will generally open up. The backside split end comes off the ball under control up to a six- to eight-yard depth at three-quarter speed. He then slants inside for another five yards before turning upfield at approximately the hash mark. It is vital that he run directly up the field and not drift in toward the safety. He looks for the ball over the inside shoulder (Diagram 5.14).

The seam-post has produced many big plays. The key is to make sure that it is no more than an eighteen- to twenty-yard pass. If the split end is too far downfield, he must slow down the first two cuts of the route.

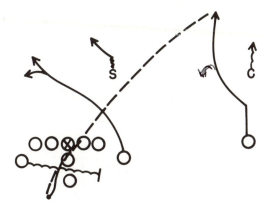

Diagram 5.14 Throwback, Option Five

The five-under, two-deep coverage is becoming more common and can be an effective defense. But like all defenses the ability of the defensive backs determines how strong the defense will be. With sting the defense is often stretched to its breaking point with the three-deep options forcing a three-on-two in the deep zones (Diagram 5.15). If the secondary rolls toward the quarterback drop, the backside split end has the option of curling his seam-post into the deep middle hook area, under the safety and between the dropping linebackers (Diagram 5.16).

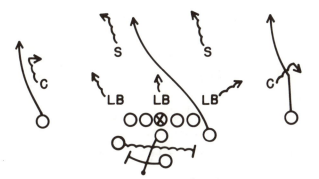
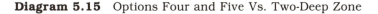

Diagram 5.15 Options Four and Five Vs. Two-Deep Zone

Note: **When the slotback reads a five-under defense, he will automatically run the deep option.**

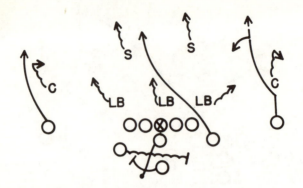

Diagram 5.16   The Curl Option

> *Note:* **The backside split end has the option of the curl route against the two-deep secondary.**

The Delay (Option 6)

The motion slot has a dual responsibility during the play. First, on the snap he pass-blocks the backside defensive end. After blocking for a three-count, he releases the end to the outside and drifts to the open area left by the drop of the linebackers. Turning back to face the quarterback, he becomes the under-coverage receiver (or safety valve) if all other options are covered (Diagram 5.17).

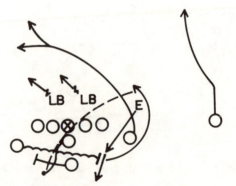

Diagram 5.17   Slot Delay, Option Six

The Quarterback Read

Although the quarterbacks are taught how to identify the defensive coverages, and although the scouting report should give them an idea of what to expect, they do not actually read the coverages on the move. The quarterback makes a presnap read that gives him an idea of what the coverage might be, but after the snap he always follows his designed sequence.

Because the quarterback is going to throw to the first open receiver, it makes no difference what coverage the defensive secondary is playing. The quarterback will not be distracted or confused by attempting to read the coverage and is therefore free to concentrate on throwing the football. His instruction on sting, as on all patterns, is to throw the ball to the *first* open receiver throughout his sequence. For sting the quarterback simply looks at the onside split end, and, if he is open on the speed cut, he releases the ball on his third step, anticipating the cut of the receiver and leading him into the sideline away from the defensive back. If the quarterback sees that the out is covered, he continues his five-step drop and throws to the first open receiver from Options 2 through 6.

It is possible to predetermine the receiver in the huddle; for example, the quarterback might say, "Sting-delay" or "Sting-seam-post." The play seems to work best, however, when the quarterback reads the receivers after the snap of the football.

Practicing Sting

The best practice routine is to teach each route separately before putting the pattern together. First, run the pattern against no defense with four quarterbacks throwing at the same time, each to a different receiver (Diagram 5.18). Progressing further, run the pattern against a loose-playing secondary, and throw all six options in sequence. Finally, run the pattern against a full-speed defense and throw to the first open receiver.

> *Note:* **When going full speed, have the defense play full speed to the ball, but never have them tackle the receiver after he catches the pass.**

This is the first pattern put in the offense each year and it will be run an average of eight to ten times a game. All in all, the sting has proven to be a highly productive play. It has become the play the opponents must defend first.

> *Note:* **Have only one quarterback call the cadence, and sometimes line up the motion slot in the snap position to save time. Each quarterback makes his full drop and looks at each receiver in succession before throwing to his predetermined receiver.**

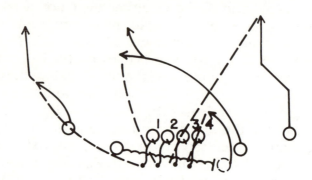

Diagram 5.18   Sting, in Practice

The quarterbacks rotate from left to right, staying in the same position for two repetitions. The receivers return to their position lines, being careful not to run back through the drill. The first quarterback throws to the frontside split end, the second quarterback to the stationary slotback, the third quarterback to the backside split end, and the fourth quarterback to the motion slotback.

Chapter

6

The Short Passing Game

A good passing team is able to attack the entire defense and to throw both long and short. It uses play action passes and has a sound screen and draw plan. Further, a really good passing team beats the defense by stretching it both horizontally and vertically. The short passing game is designed to attack the soft underbelly of the defense. To spread the defense, use alignment and motion. Stretch it vertically with the threat of deep receivers, and then hit under the defensive backs with short, crisp patterns. Although this chapter deals with the short passes, yardage is not limited to short gains. In fact, many big plays have come on short passes that have turned into long touchdowns.

This chapter covers the short patterns called first down, cardinal, Stanford, and hot; details the short option; and describes the combinations. The coaching method involves first teaching individual routes and then combining them into patterns with two or three receivers.

First Down

The term *first down* tells all receivers to run the inside curl route. It is a good idea to add motion with the backside slotback (Diagram 6.1).

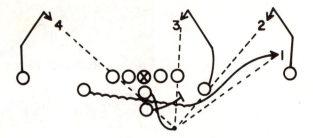

Diagram 6.1   First Down Flood: "18 Rip, First Down, LH Flood"

If the slotback is in rip or wiz motion, call his pattern. However, in roar or wham motion he automatically runs the bubble route unless told otherwise (Diagram 6.2).

The quarterback takes a five-step drop and throws to the first open receiver from Options 1 to 4.

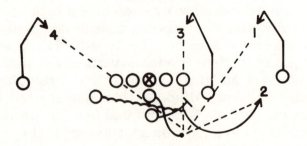

Diagram 6.2   First Down, Bubble: "18 Roar, First Down"

Cardinal

Although cardinal can be thrown to the frontside, it is best run as a throwback. This play was adapted to the offense from a similar play picked up during a clinic at Stanford University, thus the name *cardinal* (Diagram 6.3).

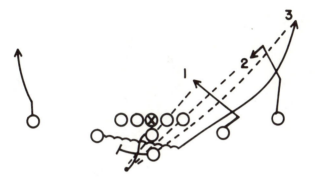

Diagram 6.3   Cardinal

The stationary slotback is the primary receiver and is most often open at about a five-yard depth. He must begin a flood route and wait for the motion slotback to pass before cutting under him and turning upfield, being careful not to run too far into the middle where the linebackers are generally waiting. If the stationary slotback is covered, the backside split end will usually be open after the slotback passes through the quarterback's line of vision.

> *Note:* **It is important for the split end to time his pattern so as not to make his break back toward the quarterback until just after the slotback clears the area.**

The third option is for the motion slotback to run a flood-and-up route, making sure that he is outside the split end before he turns upfield. This option can break wide open if the defensive corner plays the split end curl too close.

The frontside split end is free to run any route as a decoy, usually an up, seam-post, or curl.

Stanford

This is another play picked from Stanford's pocket. It may be run from the double slot (Diagram 6.4) or from a broken formation (Diagrams 6.5 and 6.6). The latter is described in chapter 13.

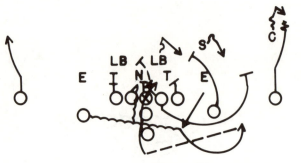

Diagram 6.4   Stanford: "16 Roar, Buck Right, Stanford Right"

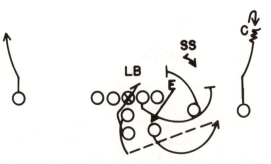

Diagram 6.5   Stanford, With Play Action: "Wide 46, Buck Right, Stanford Right"

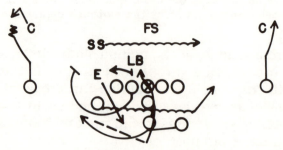

Diagram 6.6   Backside Stanford: "57 Rip, Buck Left, Stanford Left"

Because of a strong rotation toward motion, Stanford can be a very effective play to run away from the motion slotback.

When Stanford is run toward the stationary slotback, that player releases outside the defensive end and turns inside to block the first linebacker. Because the pass is behind the line of scrimmage, it is legal to block downfield. The frontside guard pulls and, while avoiding the defensive end, turns up-field and blocks the force man. The fullback buck fake tends to keep the linebackers from pursuing too quickly and gives the guard time to get in front of the motion back. The quarter-back must gain depth as quickly as possible to create distance from the unblocked defensive end and to flip a short forward pass over or around him. Stanford is a very effective and quick screen-type play that seems to work best on first down.

Hot Pass

The *hot pass* is a simple play that works great against teams that like to blitz or run man-to-man defenses. The quarter-back has four options, all of which can be executed within a three-step drop (Diagram 6.7). It will require that the quarter-back make a presnap read of the defense to determine where he will likely throw the football.

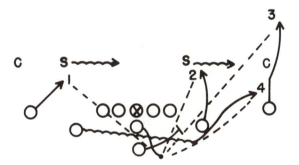

Diagram 6.7   Hot Pass Options: "16 Rip, Hot Pass Right"

If the defensive safety moves to the middle with motion, the quarterback's first option is the throwback slant. If he doesn't like the slant, he then looks for the stationary slot on the quick pop pass. If the defense is playing tight, the quarterback may decide on the quick up to the frontside split end. Finally, if everything else is covered, he will drop the ball to the motion back on the flood route. Because Options 2, 3, and 4 are all on the frontside in the same line of vision, it is relatively easy for the quarterback to make the right decision on where to throw the football. Adding play action in this situation helps hold the linebackers (Diagrams 6.8 and 6.9).

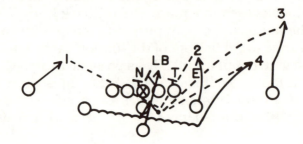

Diagram 6.8   Play Action, Hot: "16 Rip, Belly Right, Hot Pass Right"

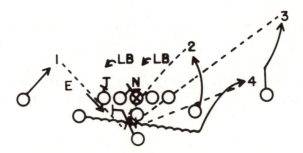

Diagram 6.9   Hot, Play Action Backside: "17 Rip, Belly Left, Hot Pass Right"

Short

Short is a version of scramble (chapter 5). As in scramble, short allows the receiver to read the defense and run any short pattern. He must make his final break at the count of three. Short can be thrown to the two-receiver side (Diagram 6.10) or called to an individual receiver (Diagrams 6.11 and 6.12). The quarterback has the option of using the three- or five-step drop (Diagrams 6.10 to 6.12).

Note: **The other receivers execute deep decoy routes.**

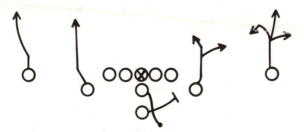

Diagram 6.10   Frontside Short: "18 Short"

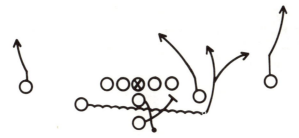

Diagram 6.11   Motion, Short: "18 Rip, LH Short"

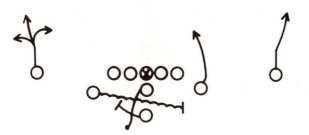

Diagram 6.12   Motion Opposite, Short: "19 Rip, LE Short"

Combinations

By combining short patterns with throwback patterns (chapter 7), you can develop an excellent sequence (Diagram 6.13).

By using your imagination you can design many different combinations that can be effective and worthwhile.

Combining the short pattern with the throwback pattern gives the quarterback another option if the short pattern is well covered (Diagrams 6.14 and 6.15).

Combining two short routes is also possible. Sting and cardinal can be combined to give defenses fits (Diagram 6.16).

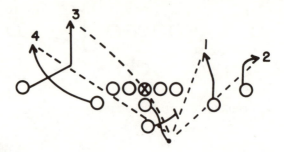

Diagram 6.13   Route Combinations: "Wide 18 Hot Pass, RE Sting, Throwback Switch"

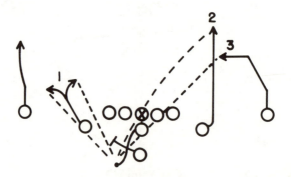

Diagram 6.14   Combinations: "19 LH Short, Throwback Touchdown"

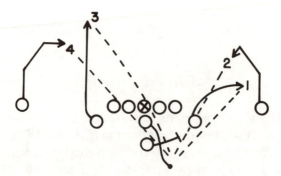

Diagram 6.15   Combinations: "18 First Down, RH Flood, Throwback Touchdown"

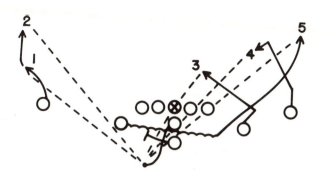

Diagram 6.16   Sting to Cardinal: "19 Rip Sting, Throwback Cardinal"

Summary

These five pass plays with combinations plus sting (chapter 5), double-up, and throwback x (chapter 8) provide an excellent assortment of short pass plays. Although the double slot is known as big-play offense, what many people forget when planning their defense is that many of the big plays come on short passes and not on the bomb.

Being able to throw short effectively also makes it almost impossible to mount an effective pass rush. The short passing game has in effect helped the overall pass game by making teams hesitant to blitz. This allows more time to throw the ball deep when choosing to do so.

As lengthy terminology can become a problem it may be necessary to use a quarterback wristband, with plays listed by number. This practice is commonly used by both college and pro teams to make it easier for the quarterback to remember and call the more complicated plays.

Chapter

7

The Long
Passing Game

To have a complete offense it is necessary to be able to throw the long pass effectively. Although it is not necessary to make the long pass a steady diet, it must be thrown often enough to force the defense to honor its threat. The effective long pass threat forces the defense to play deeper or to add an additional defensive back, both of which help open up other parts of the offense. Although there is some risk in sending four receivers into the patterns, this risk can be minimized by using discretion, and the result can be devastating to the opponent.

Some coaches believe in the theory of sending one receiver on a deep pattern and keeping everyone else in to block. Because the double slot offense has the ability to send four receivers into the pattern, the defense is forced to honor all four threats. Therefore the one-receiver philosophy is not in the double slot playbook. Four receivers at one time stretch the defense to the point where there are many holes in the secondary. This chapter diagrams the five basic long passes and shows you how to attack the defense effectively with the bomb. It also covers the sprint-out quarterback action as well as describing how to combine patterns in the long passing game.

Touchdown

All five of the long pass patterns can be either frontside or throwback passes and run with or without motion. The *touchdown* pattern has been most effective when used as a throwback pattern opposite long motion (Diagram 7.1). It often creates an overload on the throwback side with three receivers against two pass defenders. The defense is forced to drop off a backside end or linebacker to cover the pattern adequately.

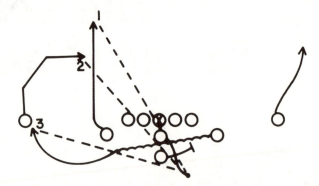

Diagram 7.1   The Touchdown Pattern: "18 Wham, Throwback Touchdown"

The first option is for the stationary slotback to run an up. It is important that the slotback take an outside release, around the defensive end, and stay on a path near the hash mark, through the seam of the defense. He must keep from drifting in toward the safety in a zone defense. The slotback must not be in too big a hurry with his release off the line of scrimmage. If his timing is right, he will break open behind the rotating safety at about a fifteen-yard depth.

The second option is for the backside split end to run a crossing pattern under the stationary slotback at about a twelve-yard depth. The split end must time his inside cut so that he reaches the point of crossing the slotback's path *after* the slotback has cleared the area. He must give the defense time to react to the up route of the slotback, therefore stretching the defense and creating a hole in the secondary.

The third option is the motion slotback on the bubble route. If the backside corner has followed the split end across, the motion back will be wide open.

This play has proven to be a great third and long pattern, especially the second option, which seems to break open with regularity.

Switch

Generally, *switch* is run to both sides at the same time, and the quarterback looks first to the frontside and then to the throwback. However, it has also been effective strictly as a throwback pattern (Diagram 7.2).

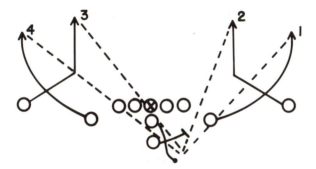

Diagram 7.2 The Switch Pattern

The split end route will usually open up against a zone defense and it is often the slotback that breaks clear against a man-to-man defense.

The split end runs a slant-and-up route that will generally be very close to the hash mark. After he turns upfield it is important for him to stay on line and not drift in toward the middle of the field. He should look for the ball over the inside shoulder at about an eighteen- to twenty-yard depth.

The slotbacks run fly routes that cross behind the split end routes. They should pass just behind the slant path of the split end, continue to widen and turn upfield near the sideline, and look for the ball over the inside shoulder at about a fifteen- to eighteen-yard depth. The quarterback takes a five-step drop and throws to the first open receiver from front to back. The receivers have the option to curl the route if the defensive secondary is playing too deep (Diagram 7.3).

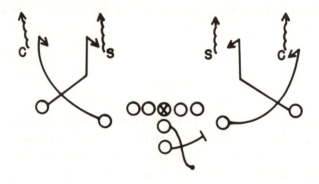

Diagram 7.3   Switch-Curl Option: "18 Switch, Throwback Switch"

It is possible to call "switch-curl" in the huddle, but generally it is more successful to allow the receivers the curl option as the play develops.

Corner

This pattern puts a lot of pressure on the defensive corner. It works very well with either no motion or long motion and is almost always thrown as a frontside pass (Diagram 7.4).

Corner with no motion is usually combined with throwback touchdown for the backside receivers (Diagram 7.5).

The frontside split end runs a bench route. He releases as if he were going to run the up, and at a ten-yard depth he turns out toward the bench and hooks back toward the quarterback.

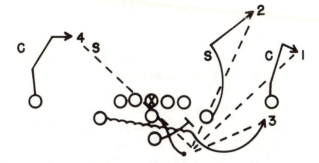

Diagram 7.4   Corner, With Motion: "18 Roar, Corner" (The QB reads the drop of the defensive corner, thus the name *corner* for this vertical stretch pattern.)

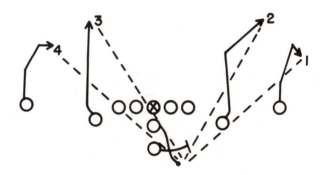

Diagram 7.5   Corner in Combination: "18 Corner, Throwback Touchdown"

He is the first option. The frontside slotback releases upfield and at the ten-yard depth cuts toward the flag on what is called a *flag route* for the slotback. Many times he will be open behind the corner, who is preoccupied with the split end. He is the second option on the corner pattern (Diagram 7.5). The motion slotback runs his bubble, being careful not to cross the line of scrimmage as that would crowd the pattern. He is the third option. The fourth option is to have the backside split end run a cross-route.

> *Note:* **Anytime a backside pattern is not called in the huddle, the backside split end runs the cross-route. This gives the quarterback one final option.**

Bingo

Bingo is called the playground play because it requires everyone to go deep, just like on the playground. All four receivers run up routes, and the quarterback throws to the open receiver. As in switch the receivers have the option to curl their route if the defense is playing too soft.

Against a three-deep secondary, the quarterback keys the safety and throws to one of the slotbacks. It works best if he pump-fakes to the frontside slotback, to influence the safety, and throws to the backside slotback (Diagram 7.6).

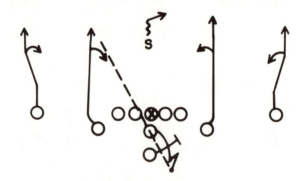

Diagram 7.6   Bingo: "18 Bingo"

Fly

The *fly* is similar to the switch in that it involves two crossing receivers. The difference is in the release off the line of scrimmage. On fly the receivers release straight off the line, and at five to seven yards upfield the split receiver runs the seam-post route. The slotback breaks to the outside, behind the split end, widens toward the sideline, and looks over his inside shoulder (Diagram 7.7). The backside receivers are free to run scramble routes.

Fly can be a frontside or a throwback pattern, with or without motion (Diagram 7.8). Adding a flood route by the stationary slotback is a good third option.

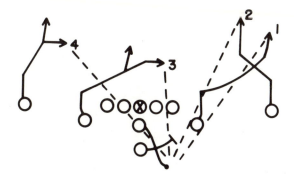

Diagram 7.7   Frontside Fly: "18 Fly"

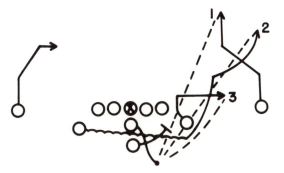

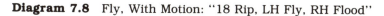

Diagram 7.8   Fly, With Motion: "18 Rip, LH Fly, RH Flood"

Sprint Out

With some quarterbacks the threat of running can make the *sprint out* a big part of the pass offense. On sprint out, hook-block the defensive end with the fullback and deepen the quarterback drop slightly to help him get outside. Sprint out can be a better play from the two-back set (Diagram 7.9).

The first option on sprint out is the pattern called in the huddle. The second option by the quarterback is to run the football. The sprint out action gives the offense a real threat of both run and pass on the corner.

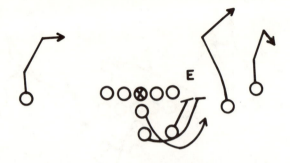

Diagram 7.9   Sprint Out Action: "Wide 48 Sprint Out, Corner"

Combinations

The system has enough flexibility to combine any frontside pattern with any backside pattern. In chapter 6 short passes were combined with long pass patterns. It is also possible to combine long passes frontside and backside. It may look complex to the opponents, but it is actually a simple system that can be very effective. Three of the better long combination routes are described in Diagrams 7.10 to 7.12.

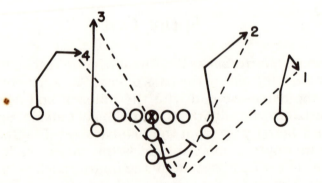

Diagram 7.10   Long Combinations: "18 Corner, Throwback Touchdown"

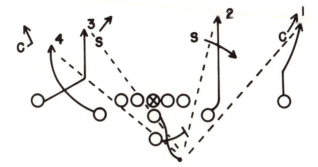

Diagram 7.11 Bingo/Switch Combination: "18 Bingo, Throwback Switch"

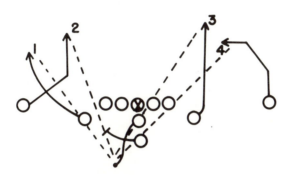

Diagram 7.12 Touchdown/Switch Combination: "19 Switch, Throwback Touchdown"

> *Note:* **Be sure that the quarterback does not predetermine his receiver. He must follow the sequence to make the play most effective.**

If the defense is in a zone coverage on the frontside, it is possible to break the slotback wide open straight down the middle of the defense (Diagram 7.11).

Put any combination of patterns together and try them in practice. Don't be afraid to listen to the players. Our own players have many times come up with outstanding suggestions.

Chapter
8

Goal Line Pass Offense

How many times have you found yourself down on the goal line with a third and six or eight and said, "What do we do now?" All the great pass patterns aren't so good when the field is shortened and there is not enough room to run deep clear-outs or crossing patterns. This chapter deals entirely with the goal line pass offense. From practice routine to individual routes to full patterns, it gives you some ammunition for the goal line.

Our quarterback coach no longer coaches a defensive position. Therefore, he works on goal line pass offense during defensive drill time. If you don't have that luxury, be sure to add some time to your offensive practice plan to work on the goal line pass (Thursday is a good day). We take all quarterbacks, backs, and receivers who don't play defense and use this period exclusively for goal line pass drills and patterns. It is important to use the actual goal line area; use the area from the five-yard line in for your practice area. If the end zone area is not free for your practice, use cones to simulate the end zone.

Warm-Up Patterns

Warm up with the quarterbacks throwing the split end double up, sting, curl, and throwback x patterns. Without using defensive backs, first work to the right and then to the left. All receivers, regardless of their actual positions, run the split end routes (Diagram 8.1).

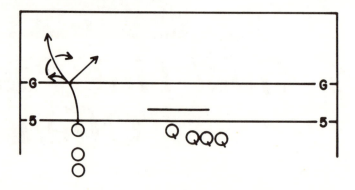

Diagram 8.1   Goal Line Pass Warm-Up Drill

Place the ball on the five-yard line in the middle of the field. Each quarterback has a ball and throws in rapid succession using the standard cadence. Each quarterback should get in as many passes as possible during this period. It is necessary to have three to five quarterbacks and eight to ten receivers who are not playing defense.

A common practice is to have the second string quarterback be a defensive starter. In order for him to get some throwing in during this time, borrow him from the defense for fifteen or twenty minutes.

As the defensive period lasts one hour (usually broken up into twenty-minute blocks), this gives plenty of time for a warm-up of about fifteen minutes. Each quarterback should throw forty-five to fifty times during the goal line warm-up. The coach stands on the endline, on or near the hash mark, so that he can see both the quarterback and the receiver.

For the next fifteen minutes add a defensive back, playing a typical goal line man-to-man defense. Signal the pass route from the position on the endline. This is a very competitive period. Try to run seven minutes on each side, with a one-minute break to change sides. Players should pair up and alternate from receiver to defensive back.

Once a week, warm up using the slot routes of throwback and slots cross. This is a good change up for the players.

For the next fifteen minutes run the complete pattern against no defense. If enough players are available, run both sides at the same time using two quarterbacks. If not, run one side at a time (Diagram 8.2).

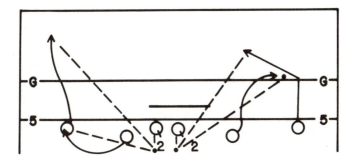

Diagram 8.2   Combination Warm-Up: "Double-Up, Throwback X"

During the last fifteen minutes add a defensive secondary and run a regular full-speed (no tackling) drill giving the offense four downs to score. Again, make this very competitive by having each team play offense and defense.

Double-Up

The split end breaks upfield for three steps before drifting outside, all the time looking back over his inside shoulder. He should catch the ball in the corner of the end zone. The quarterback should aim the ball at the flag, over the head of the defensive back.

Note: **This route is commonly called a *fade* in football terminology.**

The fifteen yards from the five-yard line to the end line is the perfect distance. If the quarterback takes too long to release the ball, the split end will run out of the end zone. Sometimes the coach stands about four yards from the sideline and endline with his hands over his head. This helps the quarterback put the correct trajectory on the ball and forces the split end to look through arms to see the ball. It is amazing how fast the quarterback learns to put the ball right on the money, and how fast the receivers learn to catch the ball at its highest point (not unlike rebounding in basketball) and get a foot down inbounds. This is a simple pattern that may be used any place on the field.

The slotback releases outside and loses ground as he runs. This is the bubble route. He should time the turn upfield so as to be on, but not over, the line of scrimmage when the ball arrives. Because the slotback is the second option on the play, the timing is more important than the speed! The quarterback takes his two-step drop (chapter 4) while looking at the split end; if he decides not to throw the first option, he takes one more step back and throws to the slotback on the bubble.

Throwback X

If the quarterback decides the slotback is not open on the bubble, he shuffles away from the line of scrimmage and turns to the backside, where he can hit the backside split end on the five-yard slant or the backside slotback on the flood.

The *throwback x* is a part of the double-up pattern. Have the quarterback call throwback x after double-up to remind the backside end and slotback of their patterns. The throwback x may be called as an individual pattern, in which case the frontside split end and slotback are free to run any route.

On throwback x the split end comes off the ball straight up-field at about three-fifths speed. He starts to drift outside as if to run the double-up. When the defensive back turns his hips to cover the up, the split end cuts inside at a forty-five-degree angle (or slant). This usually puts him at a seven- to ten-yard depth. The slotback takes an outside release, around the defensive end. He then turns upfield at three-fifths speed as if to run a seam route. At a depth of approximately five yards, he cuts behind the split end, running full speed to the sideline and looking over his outside shoulder, on what is called a flood route. Because the slotback is the last option, timing is more important than speed!

It is surprising how many times one receiver or the other is wide open on this simple route. Throwback x is a great goal line pass, whether it is part of double-up or called by itself.

Note: **The quarterback sequence for double-up, throwback x is (a) fade, (b) slot bubble, (c) slant, (d) flood.**

Sting, Goal Line

An excellent goal line play is sting, with a minor adjustment.

The Speed Cut (Option 1)

The onside split end's speed cut out is the same route as a regular sting. Most teams play a tight, man-to-man defense on the goal line, with the defensive back standing inside of the split receiver and facing out. In fact, with the double-up threat so prevalent, the speed cut option is often wide open. Be sure to have your quarterback throw the ball low and away from the defensive back. If he misses the pass, it should be too far, never behind the receiver. That interception will be 100 yards long and six points for the wrong team. Proper practice will quickly ensure that your quarterback will throw the ball in the right place.

It is after the first option that, because of the endline, the play changes (Diagram 8.3).

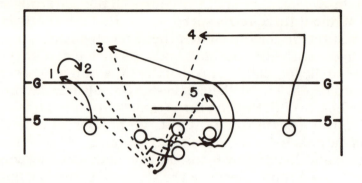

Diagram 8.3　Sting, Goal Line Pattern

The Curl (Option 2)

If the first option is not open, the quarterback pump-fakes on his third step and continues to his normal five-step drop, looking for Option 2, the *curl*.

The onside split end, having run his speed cut and not received the ball, turns upfield on his seventh step. He then plants his left foot on his eighth step, dips his inside shoulder (have the receiver touch the grass with his inside hand), and executes a tight curl or hook (Diagram 8.4). By the eleventh step the receiver is at approximately an eight-yard depth, moving directly back to the quarterback and away from the defensive back.

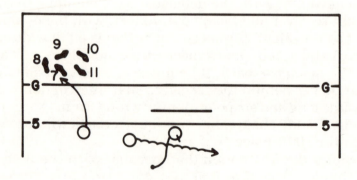

Diagram 8.4　Split End Footwork

As the defensive back has overplayed the out (otherwise the ball would have been thrown), nine times out of ten he will over-run the receiver and end up out of position behind the curl (Diagram 8.5).

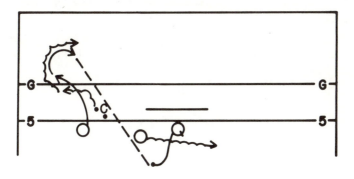

Diagram 8.5 Defensive Position

This option has proved to be excellent and is especially good against the tight-playing, aggressive defensive back.

Motion Slot (Option 3)

If the stationary slotback runs across the field as in a regular sting, he will arrive too soon. The defensive back covering the slotback can release and intercept the pass intended for the curl. Therefore, on sting, goal line, the slotbacks change assignments. The motion slotback turns upfield, outside the defensive end, and runs across the field aiming for the opposite corner. Many times the defensive back guarding him will over-run, and the slotback will be open in the back corner of the end zone (Diagram 8.3).

Endline Cross (Option 4)

The backside split end runs a double-up route and tries to drive the defensive back out of the end zone. He then turns to the inside and runs parallel to the endline. He may very well find himself open under the goal post for an easy score (Diagram 8.3).

The Delay (Option 5)

The stationary slotback lets the defensive end come to him and, protecting his inside gap, blocks the end for a three-count, releases him to the outside, and drifts to the open area, where he becomes the delay option for the quarterback (Diagram 8.3).

Over the years the sting, goal line play has become very productive. With its built-in options it has literally become five plays in one.

Slots Cross

This play was added recently, and it has been a good addition. As the name implies, it calls for the slotbacks to cross, with the backside slotback running under the frontside slotback and becoming the primary receiver (Diagram 8.6). He will be at approximately an eight- to ten-yard depth, running toward the corner of the end zone.

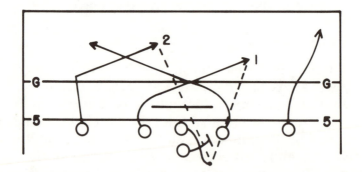

Diagram 8.6   Slots-Cross Pattern

The onside slotback continues across the field, heading for the opposite corner at a ten-yard depth.

The backside split end runs a throwback-x route and continues under the crossing slotback, who is heading for the far goal post. He is the second option. The onside split end has an important job. He must trick the defensive corner into believing he is the primary receiver. He runs a double-up route and jumps in the corner of the end zone as if to catch the ball.

As you can tell, much time is spent practicing the goal line pass offense. There is no doubt that the goal line offense can lead to great benefits, as can the entire pass offense due to the extra practice time in throwing and catching.

Goal Line Defense

The six-five is the goal line defense we see most often (Diagram 8.7). The pass-blocking rules described in chapter 3 work nicely against this defensive alignment.

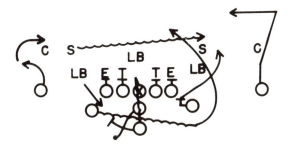

Diagram 8.7   Blocking Goal Line Sting

Against an eight-man defensive front (usually a six-two alignment), we will audible to double-up, backside x (Diagram 8.8).

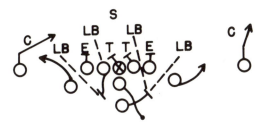

Diagram 8.8   Double-Up X

The quarterback reads the frontside linebacker; if he blitzes, he simply dumps the ball to the slot. If the backside linebacker blitzes, the slot calls "hot" and looks quickly for the ball. The fullback and backside guard have dual blocking responsibilities.

9

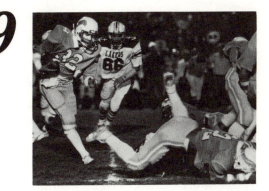

Screens, Draws, and Safety Blitzes

Any offense that relies on the pass must be able to nullify the strong pass rush. The quick passing attack (covered in chapter 6) is one method; equally important is a well-designed screen and draw plan. This chapter describes four different types of screens and two types of draw plays that diversify the offense and, at the same time, fit nicely into the double slot concept. The double slot screens and draws, as well as the techniques to teach them, are covered in this chapter. In addition, because it is very important to understand how to attack the blitzing safety, this chapter gives a sound plan to defeat the safety blitz.

Quick Screen

The first screen pass put into the offense each year is the full-back *quick screen*. This is the easiest of the screen passes to run and may be the most effective (Diagram 9.1).

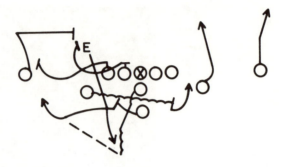

Diagram 9.1   Quick Screen: "19 Rip, RB Quick Screen Left"

The quick screen can be run either with no motion or toward motion, but most of the time it is best to run it away from motion. The backside slotback and split end run up routes, and the center and backside guard and tackle pass-block using the pass rules (chapter 3).

The play-side split end breaks off the ball as if to run an up, breaks down at about a ten-yard depth, and turns inside as if to run a crossing route. He then blocks the first opposite color with an above-the-waist stalk block.

The play-side guard and tackle pass-block for a two-count. If uncovered, they stay in place for the two-count and then release along the line of scrimmage to the outside. The tackle blocks the first opposite color to the outside, usually the corner, and the guard turns inside and blocks the first opposite color, usually the safety.

The motion slotback blocks the backside end for a three-count and then releases downfield.

The fullback attacks the play-side defensive end and blocks aggressively for a two-count. He must turn the defensive end to the outside when he releases him to give the quarterback more time to set up the screen. After releasing the end, the fullback takes a step or two away from the line of scrimmage while turning to the inside. He should be facing the quarterback as he receives the pass.

> *Note:* **Although it is somewhat faster to catch the ball over the outside shoulder and turn upfield, the play seems to be more effective when the fullback turns to the inside after catching the ball. His vision is better and he is better able to use his blockers.**

The quarterback takes his normal five-step drop and backpedals to draw the defensive pass rushers toward him. He then flips a short pass over the onrushing defensive linemen to the fullback.

This simple screen pass is a very fast-hitting play that can break for big yardage. Because of the spread-out defense against the double slot, there is often a lot of running room away from motion.

Slow Screen

The companion play to the quick screen is the *slow screen.* This is a good play even on long yardage downs when the defense is looking for screens and draws. It can be a good idea to give the quarterback the option of throwing either the quick or the slow screen depending on how the defense reacts (Diagram 9.2).

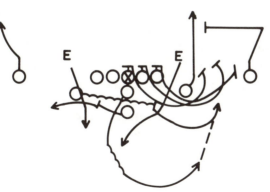

Diagram 9.2   Slow Screen: "19 Rip, Quick Screen Left, Slow Screen Right"

As in the quick screen, the play-side split end runs his crossing route and blocks the first opposite color to the inside.

The backside guard and tackle normally pass-block, and the stationary slotback and the backside split end release up-field as deep pass threat decoys.

The center, the play-side guard, and the tackle pass-block to a four-count before releasing down the line of scrimmage toward the sideline. The tackle blocks the first opposite color to the outside. The guard and center turn inside and block the first color that shows. It is imperative that the blockers wait until the ball has been caught before attacking the defense, in order to keep from getting too far downfield from the ball. If a defender reads the screen and reacts toward the pass receiver, the blockers must pick him up regardless of where the ball is at the time.

The fullback attacks the defensive end, blocks for a three-count, and releases for the fake quick screen.

The motion back blocks the defensive end for a three-count, releases him to the outside, and drifts toward the sideline behind the trio of blockers. It is very important to hide among the blockers and not be overanxious in getting to the screen area. To run the play properly, patience is a must.

The quarterback must be a real actor. He takes his normal five-step drop and backpedals for the quick screen. After faking the pass to the fullback, he wheels to the backside, turns and runs in a deep circle. This action not only causes the defensive end coming from his backside to often overrun, but also gives the appearance of panic and further draws the defensive pass rushes to the quarterback. As the quarterback circles back toward the line of scrimmage, he throws a short pass to the waiting slotback behind the three-man screen.

Note: **Always teach screen passes in a team setting. Explaining the entire play to the team seems to give everyone a better understanding of the play. Also, the timing may differ slightly and it must be worked out between the line and backs as a unit.**

The slow screen can be run by itself, but when combined with quick screen it can put tremendous pressure on the defense. Simply have the quarterback read the reaction of the defense and, if the quick screen is open, hit the fullback. If the defense has covered the quick screen, wheel to the backside and hit the motion slotback on the slow screen.

Middle Screen

Once the defenders see the quick and slow screens, they sometimes play soft on the outside, which makes it difficult to screen to those areas. The *middle screen* has enabled us to take advantage of an aggressive interior defensive line (Diagram 9.3).

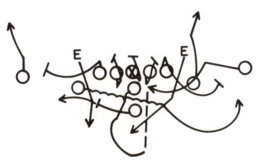

Diagram 9.3 Middle Screen: "19 Roar, Quick Screen Left, Right End Middle Screen"

Because the idea is to spread the defense, use long motion to draw the defense in that direction. By faking the fullback quick screen away from motion, the defense is spread even further, thus opening the middle area.

The play-side split end and the stationary slotback are deep decoys. The motion slotback runs his bubble route and stops to decoy a screen in that area.

The play-side tackle pass-blocks for a two-count and runs quick screen. The backside tackle pass-blocks for a four-count and runs slow screen. The center and both guards pass-block to a four-count and then form the middle screen. The guards block the first opposite color to the outside, and the fullback runs the same action as in slow screen: a three-count block on the defensive end and fake quick screen.

The backside split end shuffles down the line of scrimmage as if to crack-back-block. He must not be overanxious but should time his move to the middle after the pass rush has left the area. If he does it right, he will get lost in the shuffle of bodies and will seem to appear out of nowhere at just the right time.

The quarterback fakes the fullback quick screen, wheels around as if to run slow screen, and then passes the ball to the split end in the middle, usually three to five yards behind the line of scrimmage.

The outside decoys and the timing of the play are vital. Don't be afraid to spend some time getting it down right; the middle screen can save or break a game.

Speed Screen

The *speed screen* is another split end screen that is usually run with play action (sweep action works well). Generally, faking the sweep will draw the defense in that direction and open up the backside for the speed screen (Diagram 9.4).

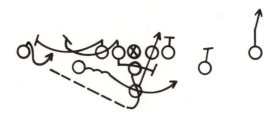

Diagram 9.4   Split End, Speed Screen: "16 Red Sweep Right, Speed Screen Left"

The backside slotback and tackle man-block. The backside guard pull- and trap-blocks, and the center also man-blocks or check-blocks against an even-man defensive line. The fullback fills for the guard or center, and the motion slotback fake-sweeps. The backside split end decoys the defensive corner.

The play-side guard and tackle block aggressively for a one-count before releasing down the line of scrimmage toward the sideline. The tackle blocks the first opposite color to the outside, usually the corner. The guard turns inside at the point of attack and blocks the first opposite color, usually a linebacker.

The play-side split end takes a step downfield and runs a tight half-circle behind the line of scrimmage, catching the ball on the run and splitting the defense between the two blockers.

The quarterback moves straight back from the center, gaining as much depth as possible, fakes to the motion slotback, and fires a quick pass to the split end behind the line of scrimmage.

Draw-Trap

Any passing team must have a good draw play to complement its pass offense. The double slot *draw-trap* has been an effective play for years. It can allow the team to break for big yardage when the defense puts on an aggressive pass rush.

Run draw-trap with no motion or back-toward motion. The defensive end away from motion many times will back off when motion occurs and will be in position to tackle the fullback. However, the defensive end on the stationary slotback side will always stay on the line of scrimmage and usually give a good pass rush. In either case he becomes no factor in the play. If the backside defensive end is consistently giving a hard pass rush the draw-trap will work nicely in either direction (Diagram 9.5).

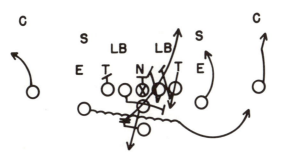

Diagram 9.5   Draw-Trap: "10 Roar, Fullback Left, Draw-Trap Right"

The line runs trap (chapter 3) after making a one-count pass-protection fake. The two split ends and the stationary slotback are deep pass route decoys.

The fullback takes one or two steps toward the defensive end and waits for the quarterback to come to him. After receiving the ball, he follows the trapping guard.

The quarterback takes his normal five-step drop, looking downfield and seeing the fullback in his peripheral vision. He must hold the ball in the same manner as he does on a pass play. As he passes the fullback, he simply slips the football into his belly and continues his pass drop.

It is possible to run the fullback draw with man-blocking. However, the trap block has proven to be much superior. With man-blocking it becomes almost impossible to run the draw against a blitz. However, with draw-trap the blitzing player often gets blocked by the trapper, resulting in a long gain (Diagram 9.6).

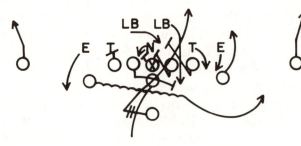

Diagram 9.6   Draw-Trap Vs. the Blitz

Lead Draw

The *lead draw* is a change-up draw that can be effective against a standard fifty defense. This play works best from the two back set (Diagram 9.7).

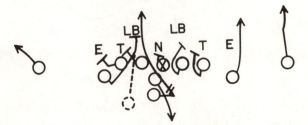

Diagram 9.7   Lead Draw: "10 (20) Fullback Right, Lead Draw Left"

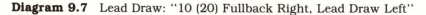

The play action by the quarterback and the fullback is the same as in draw-trap. The play-side slotback and both split ends are deep pass route decoys.

The backside guard and tackle each block one man aggressively to the outside. The backside slotback (or halfback) pass-blocks for a one-count before leading up on the backside linebacker.

Strong Safety Blitz

There are a number of ways to handle the *strong safety blitz:* (a) hold an extra player in to block, (b) use an audible and check out of a bad play, and (c) use the "hot" receiver. Simply stated, the quarterback and frontside slot key the strong safety on all frontside passes. If the strong safety blitzes, the quarterback immediately dumps the ball to the slotback on a quick look-in (hot) route (Diagram 9.8). The frontside slot releases outside the defensive end and looks for the pass over his inside shoulder. If the strong safety fakes the blitz and drops to his normal position, the players should continue with the play called in the huddle (Diagram 9.9).

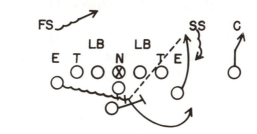

Diagram 9.8 Strong Safety Read

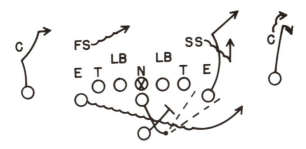

Diagram 9.9 The Fake Blitz: "18 Roar, Corner"

Free Safety Blitz

The hot receiver principle is also used to handle the *free safety blitz*. The split end away from motion keys the safety to his side. If the free safety assumes a blitz alignment on motion, the split end runs the hot route, which is a quick slant to the vacated area. If the quarterback reads free safety blitz, he takes his two-step drop and hits the split end on the quick slant (Diagram 9.10).

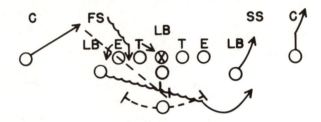

Diagram 9.10   Free Safety Blitz

If a backside pass has been called in the huddle, the fullback blocks the Number 3 defender. If a frontside pass has been called, the pass should be thrown before the free safety becomes a factor. In either case, the linemen follow their blocking rules and block their inside gap first.

This method of handling safety blitzes will take some time to learn, but once it has been covered, it is easy to perform and very effective.

Chapter

10

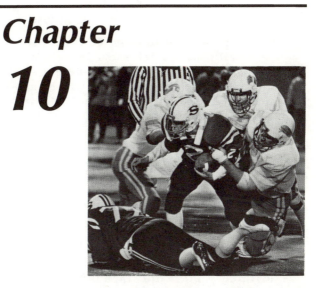

The Inside Run Offense

The double slot offense is designed to have the ability to take advantage of the weak point of the defense. In other words, this offense is able both to pass and to run the football. There are certain advantages to being known as a passing team. One is that most defensive teams will play something other than their regular defense. Another advantage is that defenses will commonly use five or six defensive backs who are designed to take away the pass. Because of the opponent's preoccupation with defending the pass, it makes it much easier to run the football.

The run offense in the double slot is a very sound concept. It has the ability to attack both inside and outside with equal ability and diversification. This chapter shows you how to attack the defense with an inside running game that not only complements the passing game and sets up the outside running game, but is in itself exciting and explosive.

> *Note:* **It would be impossible to diagram each play against all possible defenses. Therefore, blocking schemes against the three basic defenses, the 5-2, the 6-1 or 4-3, and the split four, will be shown. Many special defenses may have to be dealt with, but most of these are some version of the basic three.**

The Buck

It is very difficult to run outside unless you first establish the inside running game. The basic inside play is the fullback *buck.* The play can be run with either no motion or slotback motion of any kind.

The fullback buck may be blocked with either man- or cross-blocking, using the You or I line call (refer to chapter 3). Trap blocking gives the play still another look (see chapter 3). The buck is a simple, sound, and quick-hitting play that not only is a big gainer but sets up the buck sweep nicely (Diagram 10.1).

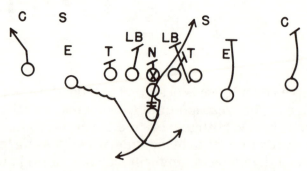

Diagram 10.1   Cross-Block Buck: "10 Red, Buck Right"

The quarterback reserve-pivots toward the play. For example, on buck right, he pivots toward the right and gets the football to the fullback as deep in the backfield as possible. This allows the fullback to read the line blocking and cut toward daylight.

If short motion by the slotback has been called, the quarter-back fakes the sweep handoff and continues a bootleg action. If not, the quarterback simply continues the bootleg action without the sweep fake.

Use the center-guard cross-block (check-block) against an even defense and always cross-block away from the play call (Diagram 10.2). The split ends run up routes after taking maximum splits to widen the defensive secondary. The stationary slotback releases outside the defensive end and blocks the safety.

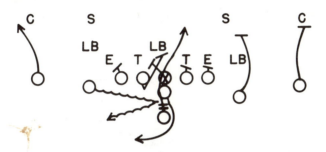

Diagram 10.2   Buck Vs. "40" Defense: "10 Rip Away, Buck Right"

Some kinds of split defenses are popular and usually balanced, as in the split four with a five-deep secondary. In those cases block away from the play call and leave the defensive man lined up outside of the play-side guard untouched. Another method is to sucker-block with the guard and bring the tackle down on the linebacker (Diagram 10.3).

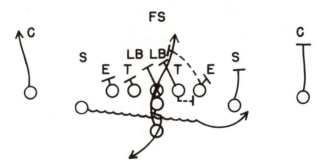

Diagram 10.3   Buck Vs. "Split" Defense

Use the trap block as a change-up. It is most difficult against an odd defense. It requires the fullback to make a sharp cut behind the line of scrimmage. It is important that the quarterback get plenty of depth before making the handoff (Diagram 10.4).

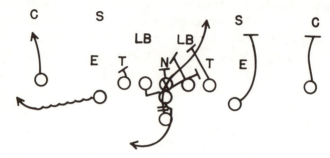

Diagram 10.4   Trap the Buck: "10 Red Away, Buck Trap Right"

The Inside Veer

Many coaches believe that you can't throw the ball and also run the option. It has been our experience, however, that you can do them both, and do them both well! It is unnecessary to spend a lot of time practicing the reading of the *inside veer*. For some quarterbacks it is a very easy read, for others it is difficult. Don't ask those quarterbacks who have a difficult time with the play to read it. It is no different from having one quarterback who is a drop-back passer and one who is a sprint-out passer. You wouldn't ask the sprint-out quarterback to throw a drop-back pass, so why ask the nonreader to read the triple option? For the quarterback who has difficulty reading the veer, it is still possible to run the play by predetermining who will get the ball.

Always block the inside veer the same way. It makes no difference whether the quarterback is reading it or not. Take a two-foot split between the center and guard and a four-foot split between the guard and tackle. The guard's rule is to block the first man on the line of scrimmage. The tackle's rule is to block the first man inside on or off the line of scrimmage. The slotback releases outside the defensive end and blocks the defensive man assigned to "force" play from outside/in.

The fullback runs on a line through the inside hip of the guard and runs to daylight.

The quarterback takes a forty-five-degree angle step, puts the ball in the stomach of the fullback, and, while looking at the second man on the line of scrimmage, rides the fullback and makes the decision to give or keep. The quarterback accelerates after making the handoff to the fullback. The only instruction to the quarterback concerning the read is to give the ball to the fullback unless the defensive key tackles him. Likewise on the option pitch, tell the quarterback to pitch the ball unless the defensive end takes the pitch man. Never make the instructions too complicated. The quarterback will never be faced with the problem of deciding what to do. For him it is simple: Keep it unless or pitch it unless.

> *Note:* **A coaching point for the option: Tell the quarterback to think *pitch* first. He will have time to react to the keep. However, if he thinks *keep* and the defensive end is blitzing he will not have time to react and execute the pitch properly, and a fumble is likely to occur.**

Because the defense will often slant toward the motion, the fullback can get big gains on the inside veer (Diagram 10.5).

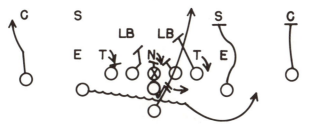

Diagram 10.5   Veer Vs. "50" Slant: "10 Roar, Inside Veer Right"

> *Note:* **The fullback's aiming point is the inside cheek of the offensive guard. He should hug the double team and move in a straight line at all times!**

If the defensive tackle moves inside the offensive tackle to the gap, the offensive tackle blocks him (see chapter 3). The fullback then veers outside the tackle's block, and the quarterback reads the defensive end as his key. In effect, the play becomes the outside veer and will almost always become a "give read" or give the football to the fullback (Diagram 10.6).

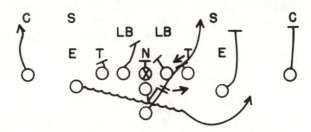

Diagram 10.6   Veer Vs. Pinch

Against a split defense, it is necessary for the center to step toward the onside gap, in case of the linebacker blitz, before blocking backside (Diagram 10.7).

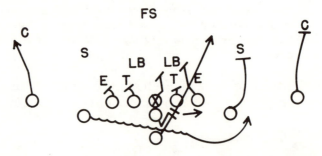

Diagram 10.7   Veer Vs. "Split" Defense: "10 Roar, Inside Veer Right"

Combo-block the frontside defensive tackle against the split look, and bounce the tackle up to the linebacker. The greatest success with the inside veer has been against the split defense. Usually the fullback will have a field day!

> *Note:*   **The slotback-block on the safety is many times a key to breaking the play for a big gain. Widen the alignment to help widen the defense.**

The Slotback Drive

The *slotback drive* is a relatively simple play that can really open up the game. When teams key the fullback and play soft outside, this play can be a game breaker. It is important that the slotback square up to the line of scrimmage before receiving the ball so he will be able to cut right, left, or straight ahead (Diagram 10.8).

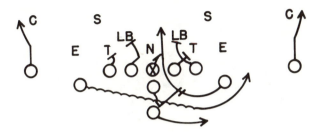

Diagram 10.8   The Drive: "10 Roar, Drive Right"

Note: Use either man- or cross-blocking with the You or I line call.

The Fullback Belly

The *fullback belly,* an inside companion play to the belly option, is a simple but good play (Diagram 10.9). Take wide splits with the offensive line, get the ball to the fullback as deep in the backfield as possible, and let him run to daylight. The fullback aims at the inside hip of the guard, but should be ready to cut right or left as daylight shows. The slotback blocks Number 3, usually the defensive end. Any line calls may be used, and the play may be run with any kind of slotback motion.

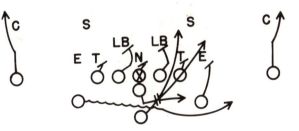

Diagram 10.9   FB Belly: "10 Roar, Belly Right"

Note: Have the quarterback accelerate past the handoff point and fake the option play.

Trap blocking is a good change-up for the belly play. It can be an explosive, quick-hitting run. On trap action have the quarterback carry out a counteroption fake (Diagram 10.10).

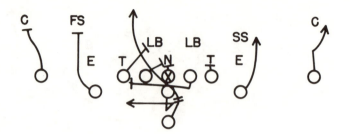

Diagram 10.10   Belly Trap: "10 Belly Right, Trap Left"

The Scissors

An excellent play from the belly series is the *scissors*. This is a quick-hitting counterplay that can completely cross up a defense. The fullback takes the belly-fake from the quarterback, and then blocks the defensive tackle. The quarterback fakes to the fullback and then makes an inside handoff to the slotback, who takes his inside release with good depth and follows the trap block of the pulling tackle (Diagram 10.11).

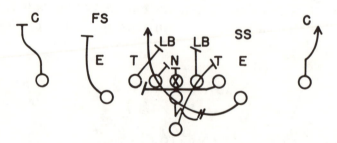

Diagram 10.11   Scissors: "10 Belly Right, Scissors Left"

By running the scissors with no motion, you ensure that the backside defensive end will stay on the line of scrimmage and allow the backside slot to block the safety (Diagram 10.11).

If the defensive end is an aggressive charger, it will work equally well with motion (Diagram 10.12).

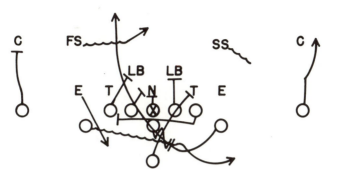

Diagram 10.12   Motion Scissors: "10 Roar, Belly Right, Scissors Left"

Although other inside running plays have been used from time to time, the five plays in this chapter are the inside bread and butter of the double slot offense. They have served us well, and they help set up the outside run offense, which will be covered in chapter 11.

Chapter
11

The Outside Run Offense

The effective running team must be able to attack the defense inside, outside, and with misdirection. This chapter covers the outside run offense from the double slot. The five outside runs consist of a crossing action, a misdirection, an option, and two power plays. These five wide-action plays have given the offense flexibility and have enabled it to attack any defense from sideline to sideline with the run.

The Buck Sweep

By first establishing the fullback buck, you force the defense to play honest. When the defense closes in to stop the fullback, it is time for the *buck sweep*.

The backfield action is the same as in the buck. The motion slotback aims for the tailback position (chapter 1), and the fullback runs the buck, making the same cut and blocking the backside linebacker. The quarterback gives an open hand to the fullback and, gaining depth, hands the ball to the motion slotback as deep as possible in the backfield. The stationary slotback doubles down with the tackle and bounces to the frontside linebacker with a combo-block (chapter 3).

Both guards pull to lead the sweep. The frontside guard seal-blocks the defensive end, and the backside guard deepens as he reaches the corner and blocks the defensive force. The backside tackle pulls and covers for the backside guard, clipping in the legal clip zone if necessary (Diagram 11.1). The combo-block by the frontside slotback makes the defensive end easy to seal-block, and the play seems to be more effective when blocked in this manner. Of course, other blocking schemes can be equally as effective.

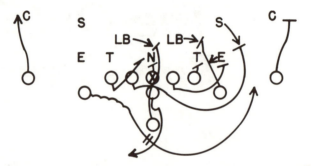

Diagram 11.1   Blocking Scheme Vs. 5–2 Defense

Against an even-man defensive front, the center fills for the frontside guard, and the backside tackle reach-blocks the defensive tackle (Diagram 11.2).

The crossbuck action of the fullback and motion slotback helps keep the linebackers at home. The fullback lead sweep can be used, but the buck sweep has been far superior. Against the split defense it is necessary to make a slight blocking adjustment with the onside guard and the slotback (Diagram 11.3).

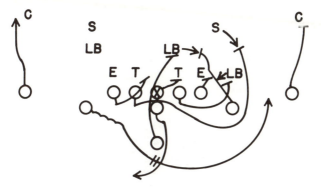

Diagram 11.2   Blocking Scheme Vs. 4–3 Defense

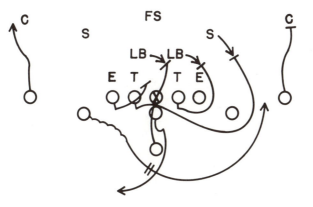

Diagram 11.3   Blocking Scheme Vs. Split Defense

The Counter

The counter has proven to be the best running play from the double slot formation. It not only gives the offense a great misdirection play, but, when used without motion, becomes a misdirection power sweep. It requires good timing and linemen who can run. With practice it can be a great addition to the offense.

The frontside guard and tackle man-block. The center manblocks against the fifty defense and checks for the backside guard against the even and split defenses. The backside guard pulls and blocks, at an inside-out angle, the defensive end. If no defensive end appears, he turns the corner and seal-blocks the first man inside. The backside tackle pulls and turns up inside the block of the guard and seal-blocks the first opposite color (Diagrams 11.4 and 11.5).

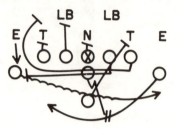

Diagram 11.4   Counter Vs. Backside Rush

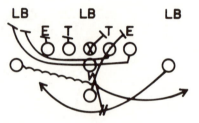

Diagram 11.5   Counter Vs. Soft Backside

The fullback runs the inside-veer angle, turns outside after the ride with the quarterback, and check-blocks for the tackle. He may align himself slightly deeper to allow the tackle to pull in front of him.

The quarterback makes the ride with the fullback as deep in the backfield as possible, pulls the football, and steps straight back for the handoff to the slotback, aiming at a depth one yard behind the fullback's feet. If he is too shallow, he will get caught up in the line action or be unable to make a sharp upfield cut inside the block of the offensive guard (Diagram 11.6).

If the frontside defensive tackle causes problems for the play, run the counter with no motion and double-team with the slotback. It is a good idea to introduce the play each year with no motion. This helps the slotback learn his blocking assignment (Diagram 11.7).

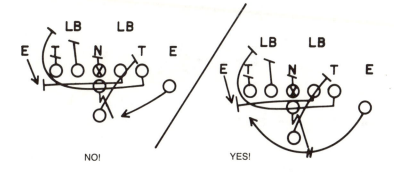

Diagram 11.6   Slotback Depth

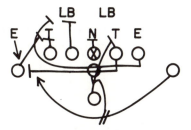

Diagram 11.7   No Motion Blocking Scheme

Although the counter can be run with motion against the split defense, it is sometimes a better play when run with no motion. With motion the play may get too congested, especially if the defense end and the tackle are good players. Block this defense two ways, depending on the alignment of the linebackers (Diagrams 11.8 and 11.9). If the linebackers are in a blitz position, down-block against the normal-depth linebacker position, combo-block the defensive tackle and the linebacker.

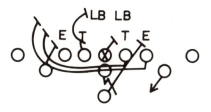

Diagram 11.8   Combo-Block

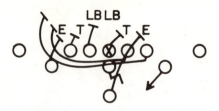

Diagram 11.9 Down Block

As a surprise play, to keep the defense honest, try running counter-keep, which is counter for everyone. The only difference is that the quarterback fakes to the slotback and keeps the ball. This is a great play against the defense that keys line-pulls and pursues toward the counteraction (Diagram 11.10).

At times changing the look of the counter by using sweep action in the backfield can work very well. The quarterback fakes the sweep, pivots, and makes an inside handoff to the counter-slotback.

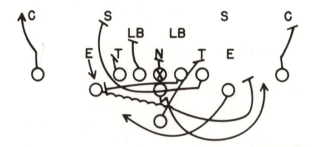

Diagram 11.10 Counter-Keep: "10 Roar, Belly Right, Counter Left Keep"

The Fullback Pitch

The *fullback pitch,* which we added in 1986, has proved to be a valuable addition to the offense. It is a power play that is especially effective against the defense that is geared to stop the pass by playing soft on the corner. Although the blocking scheme changes somewhat against different defenses, the frontside guard and motion slotback assignments, which are the key to the play, never vary (Diagram 11.11).

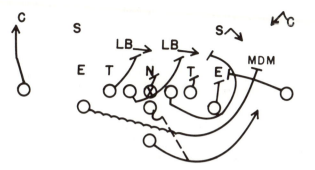

Diagram 11.11   The Fullback Pitch: "10 Rip, Pitch Right"

> *Note:* **The motion slot blocks either the safety or the corner. We refer to this position as the most dangerous man (MDM).**

This is not a sweep play; it is important that the fullback not try to outrun the defense to the sideline. Rather, he must turn upfield outside the slotback block on the defensive end and follow a straight path in the lane between the blockers toward the goal line (Diagram 11.12).

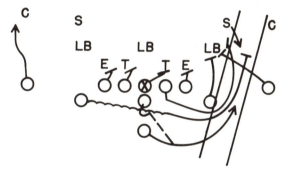

Diagram 11.12   The Fullback Pitch Path: "10 Rip, Pitch Right"

The frontside guard always pulls and turns up outside the block on the defensive end and seal-blocks—*inside.* He must resist all temptations to block the force man, whom he will nearly always see first. The motion slotback blocks the force man, usually the safety, at an inside-out angle. Against a four-deep secondary, the motion slotback cracks down the line of scrimmage with the frontside split end. He must be careful to block above the waist, and he need only pin the defensive end inside while helping the slotback. Against a five- or six-deep defense the split end stalk-blocks downfield.

The fullback must lose ground after the snap to gain enough depth to get outside the defensive end and be able to make a strong power move upfield. The quarterback reverse-pivots and makes a soft underhanded pitch to the fullback.

The blocking adjustment against the split defense involves a down-block by the stationary slotback and the onside tackle. The onside guard seal-blocks the first opposite color outside the block of the slotback (Diagram 11.13).

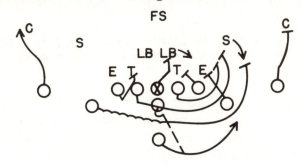

Diagram 11.13   The Path Vs. the "Split" Defense

The Belly Option

The *belly option* enables the offense to get outside quickly without blocking the defensive end. Timing is very important on this play, but when run correctly it is very difficult to defense.

The line nearly always man-blocks, and the fullback-quarterback ride is extremely important. The quarterback makes as long a ride as possible with the fullback. He should ride him into the line of scrimmage before pulling the football to run the option. Have the fullback dip his inside shoulder as the quarterback pulls the ball. This action helps hide the football and makes it appear as if he had taken it from the quarterback. After faking to the fullback, the quarterback works down the line of scrimmage and upfield toward the defensive end. As with the veer option, tell the quarterback to pitch the ball unless the defensive end takes the pitch man (Diagram 11.14).

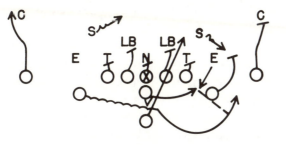

Diagram 11.14   Belly Option: "10 Roar, Belly Option Right"

The stationary slotback releases outside the defensive end and slowly advances on the safety for a stalk-block.

> *Note:* **It is important not to attack the defensive back on the stalk-block, but to settle in front of him and let the defensive back commit toward the ball carrier first. He then stays in his face and turns him to the side he wants to go. It will be up to the running back to run off the block.**

The stalk-block need only contain the defensive back long enough for the ball carrier to pass.

The split end stalk-blocks the deep-third defender, running him as deep as possible before breaking down after the defensive back reacts to the run (see stalk-blocking in chapter 2).

You can use either short or long motion for the pitch man. Long motion may provide a better pitch relationship between the quarterback and the pitch man (Diagram 11.15). The pitch man should be at least five yards outside the quarterback, and it is his responsibility to maintain the proper relationship at all times. As a change-up, cross-block between the frontside slotback and the split end (Diagram 11.15).

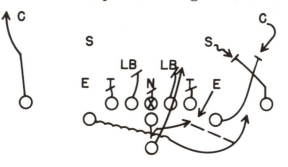

Diagram 11.15   Belly Option, Cross-Blocking

The Quarterback Sweep

If the quarterback is a good runner, the *quarterback sweep* can give the offense an excellent outside power play. Some teams will drop the outside linebacker or ends to cover the flat when they see quarterback action off the line of scrimmage. The quarterback sweep takes advantage of the softness on the corner and can turn into a consistent gain. The quarterback sweep can also be an effective way to beat the teams that consistently give a hard inside rush or blitz (Diagram 11.16).

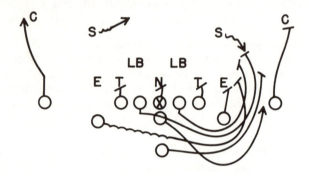

Diagram 11.16   QB Sweep Blocking: "10 Rip, QB Sweep Right"

Pull both guards against the fifty defense and seal inside after clearing the defensive end. Against a forty, the split or stack defense check-blocks with the center and pulls the backside guard only. The motion slotback doubles with the stationary slotback on the defensive end, and the fullback blocks the defensive force man. The quarterback takes his normal sprint-out drop, and, after ball-faking the pass, follows the fullback's block and heads upfield.

This play is not unlike the old single-wing sweep of years gone by and can be equally as effective.

Chapter
12

Special Plays

There will come a time when nothing in the regular offense seems to be working. At this point, the advocates of the run-a-few-plays-well theory pack their bags. This is the time to run one of the *special plays.* Sometimes it only takes one big play to rattle the defense and turn the game in your favor. Four or five special, trick, or playground plays should give your offense enough ammunition to score. The element of surprise may be enough to turn defeat into victory.

Some of these plays may be run once a game, others may be run only once a season. They have all, at one time or another, provided the one big play that enabled the offense to get moving again. In addition, once the opponents have seen these plays they must spend extra time in their practice sessions to cover them, which takes away time from learning how to defend the regular double slot offense.

P.E.

The *P.E.* play developed because of the special talent of one quarterback. It is a simple bootleg-off-the-lead sweep, with a shovel-pass option that has driven defenses crazy. In fact, the first time we ran it in a game, the fullback was thirty yards downfield before anyone knew where the ball was. The play is called P.E. because the forward lateral is part of a game played in the physical education classes (Diagram 12.1). P.E. is a fun play to execute and the first of the special plays put into the offense each year.

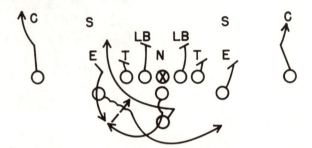

Diagram 12.1   P.E.: "10 Red, Sweep Right, Bootleg Left P.E."

> *Note:* **It is important for the fullback to stay behind the quarterback for the proper pitch angle.**

For everyone but the quarterback and the fullback, the play is sweep. Man-blocking is used, and the motion slot must do a good job of faking the sweep action. The quarterback should take a deep bootleg and not hide the ball from the defensive end. It works best when the defensive end sees the football and comes upfield across the line of scrimmage. When he does, the quarterback simply pitches the ball option-style (underhand) with a flick of the wrist to the fullback, who, after taking a lead step or two toward the sweep action, reverses direction and becomes the pitch man. In the event that the ball is dropped, it is simply an incomplete pass.

> *Note:* **Be sure to remind the officials before the game about the play. This courtesy is appreciated by officials for "trick" plays.**

If the quarterback gets around the defensive end, the play simply becomes a quarterback bootleg. The fullback turns to the inside and blocks the first opposite color (Diagram 12.2). P.E. can be run to both sides, usually at least once a game. It is a great play close to the goal line, where the defense usually loses the fullback.

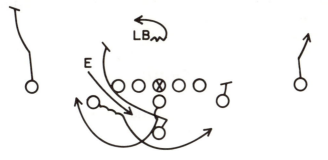

Diagram 12.2   P.E. Bootleg

Belly Keep

The *belly keep* play is designed for short yardage and is not a long gainer. It has, however, provided many big plays. Many key first downs have been made in crucial situations with belly keep (Diagram 12.3).

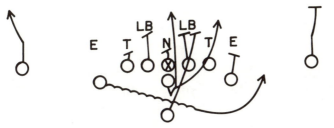

Diagram 12.3   Belly Keep: "10 Rip, Belly Right, Keep"

The tackles make the line blocking call, and the frontside slotback blocks Number 3. The fullback runs his inside-veer path and, if not tackled, blocks the first opposite color. The quarterback rides the fullback and then runs to daylight. This play has broken anywhere from back over the center to off the tackle. Also, it seems to work better when the quarterback shows good patience, makes a good ride fake, and allows the defense to overreact to the fullback or toward the option back. Some quarterbacks develop a great feel for the play and seem always to slip into the hole of the defense. The keep is an easy play to run and will provide something extra for the short-yardage offense.

Statue

The *statue* is a favorite play that has provided the offense with many big gains and has proven to be a real crowd pleaser. It is, of course, a version of the old "Statue of Liberty" play (Diagram 12.4).

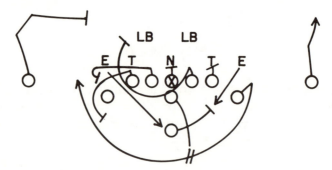

Diagram 12.4   The Statue: "10 Rip, Fullback Right, Statue Left"

Run motion, to give the backside defensive end a clear path to the quarterback. Show pass-blocking with the linemen and pull the frontside guard, who shows pass-blocking for a two-count and, avoiding the backside end, seal-blocks inside. The fullback blocks Number 3 aggressively. The quarterback takes his normal five-step drop, looking downfield, and then makes a normal handoff to the stationary slotback, who steps outside, reverses direction, and, losing ground, takes the handoff outside the quarterback at about a ten-yard depth.

Note: **By leaving the backside end unblocked, he will always go for the quarterback and arrive just after the**

handoff has been made. Of course, timing is essential, but practice time will take care of that.

Counterpass

This play can be a real game breaker and has always supplied the offense with a big play at just the right time. Of course it requires that the slotback be able to throw (Diagram 12.5).

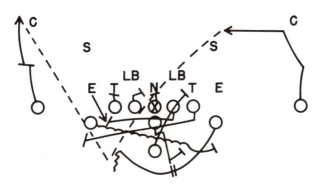

Diagram 12.5   Blocking for the Counterpass: "16 Belly Right, Counterpass Left"

> *Note:* **Sometimes substituting a quarterback for the slotback can be done, especially if the defense is used to seeing players come in and out of the game. A good time to run the play is after a change of possession when a lot of new players are entering the game on both sides.**

Pull the guard and tackle just like the regular counter. For the counterpass, however, the tackle deepens and pass-blocks at the corner. The backfield action is the same; the fullback still fills for the tackle and both the quarterback and the motion slotback pass-block on the backside. The stationary slotback must take two or three steps after receiving the handoff before pulling up inside the pocket provided by the pass-blockers and before hitting the first option, on a stalk-block and up, or the second option, on a crossing route.

> *Note:* **The frontside split end must do a great stalk-block fake. When the defensive back reacts to run, it is time to break.**

After first establishing the counter as a successful play, you can surprise the defense with counterpass, which fits in nicely with the double slot offensive concept.

Bounce Pass

The *bounce pass* looks difficult but in reality is easy to execute. Our Junior Varsity coach has run this play for thirteen years and it has nearly always been a success. It requires a good actor as the thrower and a lot of faith, but if you try it, you'll like it (Diagram 12.6).

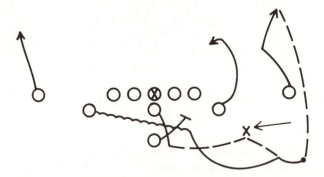

Diagram 12.6   The Bounce Pass: "18 Roar, Bounce Pass Right"

> *Note:* **Remember this is a live ball, just like any fumble.**

For the bounce pass, run long motion; the slotback must deepen more than usual on his bubble. Blocking is normal frontside and backside pass-blocking. The quarterback takes a three-step drop and throws a backward pass that must land short of the motion back. Many times it will bounce directly up to the slotback, who will then act as if it were an incomplete pass by taking a step or two before suddenly throwing a pass to the right split end, who, after first stopping, takes off for the goal line.

The bounce pass play also works very well if the ball doesn't bounce perfectly. The slotback simply ambles over to the ball lying on the turf, picks it up (in no hurry), and throws the pass. Finally, be sure to notify the officials before the game about this play. It would be a shame to have the whistle be its only defense.

The Play

Coaches and players are encouraged to come up with new special plays each week. Sometimes it is necessary to put in a special play for a particular opponent. The new play may be an end-around, a guard-special, a new screen pass, or anything. Rather than give it a name, simply call it the play. For example, instead of saying, "16 white, sweep left, reverse right, right end bench, and up," simply say, "The play, on one!" With a little imagination it is possible to come up with great plays that are effective and fun to run.

The Fullback Option

This play has become a big part of the double slot offense. It is an easy play to execute and puts extreme pressure on the defensive perimeter.

As in belly option, man-block with the frontside slotback and the split end on the defensive safety and corner, and let the tackle make the line blocking call.

The quarterback takes a two-step drop, looks downfield as if to throw a quick pass, pulls the ball down and angles for the inside shoulder of the defensive end, and executes his option. The two-step drop not only simulates pass and generally causes the linebackers and defensive backs to start their pass drops, but also allows the fullback time to get into a proper pitch relationship well in front of the quarterback (Diagram 12.7).

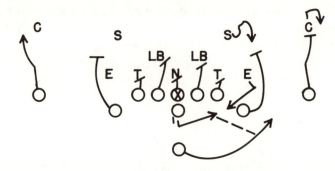

Diagram 12.7   No Motion Option: "10 Fullback Option Right"

Fullback option is a great play on the goal line, especially away from motion (Diagram 12.8). Remember that almost all goal line defenses teach the defensive linemen to stunt to the inside gap. Linemen should protect their inside gap with an aggressive down block.

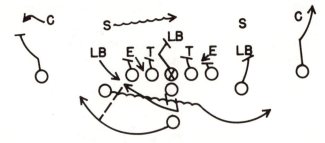

Diagram 12.8   Opposite Motion Option: "10 Roar, Fullback Option Left"

Another effective way to run fullback option is toward motion, faking the drive with the stationary slotback. Crack-back-block with the split end and lead-block with the motion slotback (Diagram 12.9).

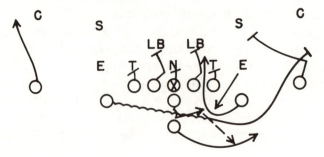

Diagram 12.9   The Drive Option

Note: **For the crack-back block to be legal it must be above the waist.**

Don't have the quarterback give a ball-fake to the slotback on "Drive." The inside action of the slotback is enough to hold the linebacker and sometimes the defensive end as well. It is not uncommon for the quarterback to get around the defensive end and option the defensive safety.

Special plays have been a big part of the double slot offense and have added a fun element that has been to the benefit of all.

Chapter
13

Break the Formation

Unless your team is simply overpowering, there will come a time during the season when the regular offense seems to be treading water. At this point you need to do something different. By breaking the formation, you force the defense to adjust to something unexpected, and this may spark your own team out of its lethargy.

This chapter covers the ways to change the formation using two back sets and overloads. These changes have caused indecision on the part of the opponents and have given the double slot offense the added firepower to break out of a temporary slump. In addition, the goal line or short-yardage set can cause defenses fits.

Two Back Set Runs

Any of the basic inside or outside running plays may be run from these formations (see chapter 1). The option plays are especially good from the two back formations. The basic belly option and the counteroption are both excellent. By using motion wisely, you can create overloads that cause all kinds of problems for the defense. The favorite option plays run from the two back formation are shown in Diagrams 13.1 to 13.4

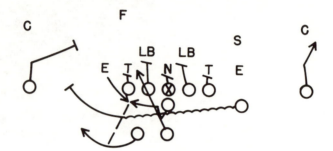

Diagram 13.1   Belly Option: "20 Wiz, Belly Option Left"

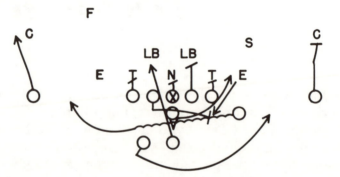

Diagram 13.2   The Counteroption: "20 Wiz, Belly Left, Counteroption Right"

Note: **On counteroption, pull the backside guard and trap-block the defensive end. The quarterback turns up inside the block and options the safety.**

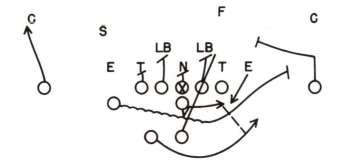

Diagram 13.3   Belly Option: "30 Rip, Belly Option Right"

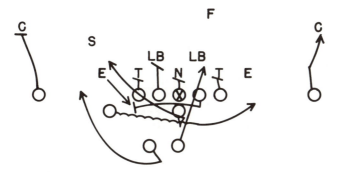

Diagram 13.4   Counteroption: "30 Rip, Belly Right, Counteroption Left"

Two Back Set Passes

The flood and throwback passes, during which the halfback comes out of the backfield, can be outstanding. This action, when used as a change-up, can cause great confusion in the defensive secondary. Two of the best plays are shown in Diagrams 13.5 and 13.6.

The two back formation has not only given real diversity to the offense, but proven to be an easy adjustment for the players and at the same time given many headaches to the opponents.

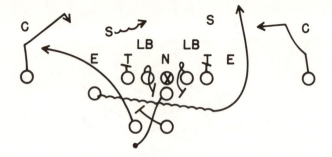

Diagram 13.5   Flood Away From Motion: "39 Rip, First Down Left Half Flood"

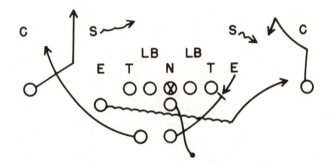

Diagram 13.6   Short Side Flood: "38 Rip, Throwback Switch"

Overload Set Runs

The overload offense has been very good for shaking up a defense and adding spark to the offense at just the right time.

The backs may be placed at any of the positions. It is possible to line up both slotbacks on the same side and move the fullback over, or place the fullback as the outside slotback and put one of the regular slotbacks at the running back position. Another way to overload is to substitute a completely new backfield. The important thing is to spend just enough practice time to make the new formation comfortable for the players. By so doing it will become an effective surprise.

Note: **For the sake of simplicity, all plays are diagrammed from the 60 formation.**

Three basic run plays are used from this formation: the toss, the outside veer, and the counter. On the toss, double-team the defensive end with the slotbacks, crack with the split end, pull the outside tackle to block force, and, using a reverse pivot, toss the ball to the running back (Diagram 13.7). All the remaining linemen pull and seal-block the first opposite color. Always run toss on a quick count to attack the defense before it has time to adjust to the offensive overload.

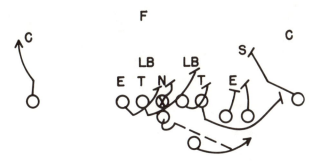

Diagram 13.7   The Toss: "60 Toss Right"

The next play is the outside veer (Diagram 13.8). The defensive end will usually move toward the outside slotback, which makes the outside veer an easy play. Base-block with the inside slotback and tackle, block the outside slotback on the strong safety, and pull and seal with the playside guard. All other linemen will man-block. The running back runs in a straight line at the outside leg of the offensive tackle. Again, run this play on a quick count.

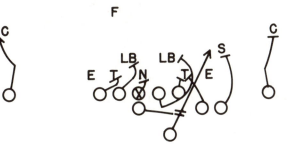

Diagram 13.8   The Outside Veer: "60 Outside Veer Right"

The regular counter works very nicely from this formation (Diagram 13.9). The only difference is that the quarterback must adjust his ride slightly because of the alignment of the fullback. Run counter on a regular snap count, allowing time for the defense to move toward the overload.

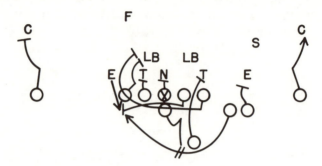

Diagram 13.9   The Counter: "60, Belly Right, Counter Left"

Overload Set Passes

By putting both slotbacks on the same side, the result is the same as when using rip or wiz motion. Any of the motion passes may be run from the overload formation. An example is shown in Diagram 13.10.

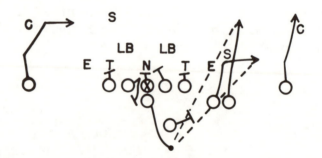

Diagram 13.10   Bingo/Flood Combination: "68 Bingo, Right Half Flood"

The two passes used most often are play action passes, from toss action. The first play action pass is shown in Diagram 13.11.

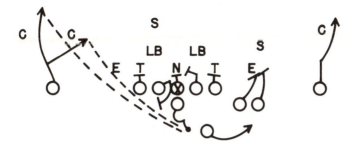

Diagram 13.11   Play Action Automatic: "1–66 Toss Right, Left End Automatic"

The quarterback makes a good toss fake with a full turn action while the running back makes an equally good play fake. The backside split end runs either a quick up or a slant, depending on the alignment of the defensive cornerback. He signals his route to the quarterback prior to the snap (any simple hand signal will do).

The second pass is the frontside play action. Use the hot pass with one small adjustment. The running back faking the toss will take the place of the flood route (Diagram 13.12).

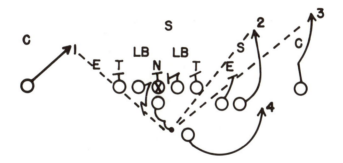

Diagram 13.12   Overload Hot Pass: "1–66 Toss Right, Hot Pass Right"

The overload hot pass play works very well against the defensive team that forces hard with its defensive backs to help stop the toss. The quarterback should get a good idea of where he will throw the ball with a presnap read of the defensive backfield alignment.

Short-Yardage Set

This is the goal line or short-yardage set. Use it when it is difficult to move the ball in short-yardage situations. Although the
formation itself goes against the wide-open nature of the offense, there is a time and place for it. As in the 60/70 series, it
is a good idea to substitute bigger players into this formation.

Six basic plays are run from the 800 set: four running plays,
the belly, the blunt, the power, and the toss; and two passes,
the power pass and double-up (Diagrams 13.13 to 13.19).

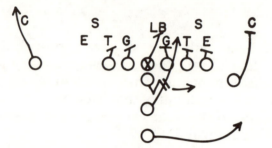

Diagram 13.13   Belly: "800 Belly Right"

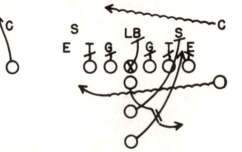

Diagram 13.14   Blunt Opposite Motion: "800 Flash, Blunt Right"

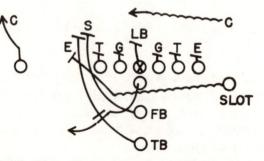

Diagram 13.15   Blunt Toward Motion: "800 Zip, Blunt Left"

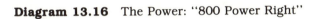
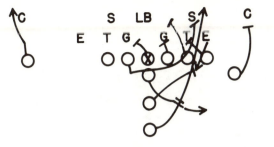

Diagram 13.16   The Power: "800 Power Right"

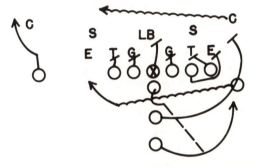

Diagram 13.17   The Tailback Toss: "800 Zip, Toss Right"

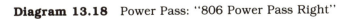
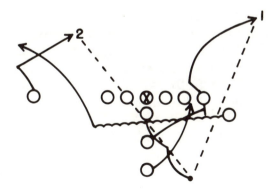

Diagram 13.18   Power Pass: "806 Power Pass Right"

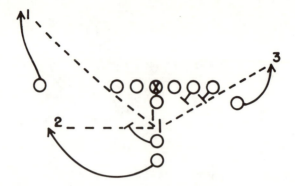

Diagram 13.19   Double-Up: "807 Double-Up"

> *Note:* **Run the fullback belly right or left, with or without motion.**

> *Note:* **Zip motion is motion with the flanker. Because this is essentially a blocking position, it is a good idea to substitute in a good blocker for zip motion.**

Man-block on the blunt play; the fullback leads through the hole to block the first opposite color. We have found that the best way to run the blunt play is toward motion. This gives the motion back a running start at blocking the defensive end and allows the fullback to lead up the hole to the first color.

Run the power only to the right, with or without motion. The backfield action is the same as the blunt. The fullback kicks out the defensive end, and the left guard leads up the hole and seals inside. This is a true power play and is a good change-up from the blunt.

The toss may be run with no motion; however, it is best when the defense runs with motion. The tight end down-blocks, and the frontside tackle pulls and reach-blocks the defensive end. The fullback leads around the corner and blocks the first color. The tailback should lose ground on the snap to gain enough depth to get around any defensive pressure on the end of the line of scrimmage (Diagram 13.17).

It is possible to run the belly option and the belly keep from the 800 set. However, the four basic power-type plays form the nucleus of the run offense at the goal line.

The play action pass is run from the power action and is a very effective play. It is best when run with motion because it gives the quarterback a second option on the backside.

The first option is the tight end in the corner of the end zone. If he is covered the quarterback will look to the backside split end on a throwback-x route, breaking under the route of the motion back (Diagram 13.18).

The double-up is only run to the left, toward the split end, and is a quarterback two-step drop. If all three receivers are covered, instruct the quarterback to throw the ball out of the end zone (Diagram 13.19).

In its pure form, the double slot offense has enough weapons to give most defensive schemes total nightmares. However, like almost any offense, it will require some adjustments as soon as defenses have had a few years to catch up. This will not be a problem if you simply use the change-ups reviewed in this chapter within the structure of the offense to extend its effectiveness.

Schedule a specific time during the practice for the added formation or play and practice it just enough to make it effective. The result will be well worth the extra time spent. We have found that the sudden use of a broken formation completely dumbfounds a defense that has been geared entirely to stop the double slot in its simple form. In short, take advantage of what the defense gives up and attack its weakness with imaginative offensive ideas.

Epilogue

Writing this book has been a very gratifying experience for me. The process was sometimes exasperating but well worth the effort. Putting thoughts down on paper can be a very revealing process. During the time I spent writing the book, I would periodically have thoughts that didn't seem to fit into a particular chapter. I would like to share them with you at this point. They are in no particular order; the list is more a random sampling of my general philosophy.

- Take the game of football seriously, but never take yourself too seriously.
- Guide them, organize them, motivate them, teach them, love them; but for God's sake, don't *overcoach* them.
- Fit the system to the personnel, not the personnel to the system.
- The biggest challenge each year is to put kids into a position where they have a chance for success.

- Never ask a kid to do something that is physically or mentally impossible for him to do, and then blame him when he can't do it.
- Honest emotion is great! Don't be afraid to be real. Never be too proud to cry!
- Be totally honest with yourself as well as with your players.
- Never allow yourself to become negative, and never put down your own players.
- The day you are no longer a positive influence on your kids is the day you should retire.

Finally, I hope that I have been able to spark some of your interest and that this book has been of some value to you. Good luck in the seasons to come!

Glossary

align   Position in relationship to next player.

alignment   Position in relationship to team.

away   Motion away from original position alignment.

backside   Players away from action of play.

backside rush   Defensive players rushing passer from behind.

base block   One-on-one individual block.

belly   Fullback inside run play.

bench route   Individual pass route to outside toward bench.

bingo pattern   All four receivers running up or fade routes.

blitz   Defensive maneuver crossing line of scrimmage after snap by linebackers or defensive backs.

blitz position   Close alignment by linebackers or defensive backs prior to snap.

blow   Inside linebacker blitz from split-defensive alignment.

bootleg action   Quarterback action opposite running back.

broken formation   Any formation other than double-slot alignment.

bubble route   Slotback individual pass route behind line of scrimmage.

buck   Fullback action over center.

cadence   Terminology used by quarterback at line of scrimmage.

cardinal pattern   Throwback routes of both slots and backside split end combined into pattern.

check block   Center blocking for pulling guard, away from play action.

clear out   Receiver or receivers running deep routes to clear short area for another receiver.

clipping   Blocking illegally from behind (in the non-clipping zone).

clip zone   Area between offensive tackles on the line of scrimmage where it is legal to block from behind.

combinations   Pass routes combined to form frontside and backside patterns.

combo-block   Blocking technique usually between guard and tackle blocking defensive tackle and linebacker.

corner pattern   Combination bench route by split end and flag route by slotback.

counter   Misdirection run by slotback.

coverage   Defensive backfield style, usually man-to-man or zone.

crack-back block   Technique whereby the split receiver blocks defender aligned inside of his position.

crossbody block   Blocking technique using a rolling attack on the defensive player.

cross-route   Ten- to twelve-yard route across formation.

cross stunt   Defensive maneuver by defensive end and outside linebacker.

curl route   Ten- to twelve-yard individual pass route, turning toward the inside.

cut block   Blocking technique used to block hard-charging defensive player by attacking him around the shin area.

cut the slack   Refers to fullback (or halfback) attacking the defensive end, under control, thereby cutting the distance between the two.

deep third defender   Defensive back assigned to one third of the field in a zone pass coverage.

deep threat   Offensive receiver running a deep route.

defensive perimeter   Referring to the defensive backs and linebackers responsible for the outside area.

delay route   Individual pass route whereby the receiver delays his route for a two- or three-count before slipping into the open area.

double slot   Basic formation or alignment.

double team   Two offensive blockers assigned to one defender.

double-up pattern   Combination of four different routes making up a pattern in the quick pass game.

down-block   Line call referring to blocking the first player inside.

downfield block   Blocking a defensive player past the line of scrimmage.

draw-trap   Fullback run after a pass action fake by the quarterback.

dual-blocking responsibilities   One offensive player assigned to two defensive players.

fade route   Terminology referring to up route.

field position   Position of football on field prior to snap.

first down pattern   Combination of routes, curl by split receiver and flood by slotback.

first opposite color   Refers to first defender to show up and be blocked.

five-step drop   Quarterback action in sprint pass game.

five-two defense   Defensive alignment with five players on the line of scrimmage and two linebackers.

five-under defense   Pass coverage with five players in the short zones.

flag route   Individual pass route toward the flag on the corner of the goal line.

flanker   Splint receiver aligned off the line of scrimmage.

flash   Fullback motion.

flood route   Short route by slotback toward sideline.

fly route   Combo pattern with crossing action between split receiver and slotback.

force   Refers to defender assigned to forcing the play from the outside in on the perimeter of the defense.

form blocking   One-on-one blocking with emphasis on technique, usually half speed.

formation   Offensive team set or alignment.

free safety   Defensive back responsible for middle of field.

free safety blitz   Attack by free safety after the snap of the ball into the offensive backfield.

frontside   The offensive side of attack.

frontside scrape stunt   Stunt involving defensive tackle linebacker crossing line of scrimmage after snap of ball.

fullback   Offensive player aligned behind quarterback.

gap call   made by offensive linemen when inside gap is threatened, calls for down block by offensive line.

give read   On veer plays, refers to action by defense requiring a give of football to fullback.

grip   Refers to quarterback holding football.

half-line   Offensive or defensive group drill involving right or left side of the line only.

hash mark   Markings on field dividing field into approximate thirds.

hook area   Area in secondary approximately ten to twelve yards deep.

hook block   Blocking technique used to keep a defensive end pinned to the inside, while ball goes outside.

hot pattern   A combination of routes by four receivers to quickly attack defense with short pass.

hot route   A quick look-in by slotback on hot pattern and against strong safety blitz.

huddle   A gathering of offensive players before aligning to receive instructions from the quarterback.

I block   Cross block between guard and tackle with tackle going first.

inside gap rule   Using down block to take care of inside gap threat.

inside handoff   Refers to quarterback handing off inside (back closer to the line of scrimmage than quarterback) on scissors or counter.

kick out block   Blocking the defensive end toward the outside.

lead draw   Pass action run by fullback with slotback or halfback lead blocking on the playside linebacker.

linebacker   Defensive player aligned off the line of scrimmage but not in the defensive secondary.

line calls   Refers to calls made by offensive tackles to determine blocking scheme.

line splits   Area between offensive linemen at line of scrimmage prior to the snap.

loop   Stunt, or angle of attack, to the outside gap by a defensive lineman.

loop blitz   Loop angle by the defensive lineman with linebacker blitzing the gap to the inside.

LOS   Line of scrimmage.

man-block   One-on-one block by offensive linemen.

man-to-man   Refers to secondary pass defensive coverage.

maximum protection   Utilizing one slotback to block instead of releasing into the pass pattern.

MDM   Most dangerous man; refers to man to be blocked.

middle screen   Pass play in middle after allowing defensive linemen to rush passer and create vacant area.

misdirection   Football ending up away from original back-field action.

motion   Refers to action across backfield prior to snap by a back, away from the line of scrimmage.

noseguard   The defensive player aligned over the offensive center.

number blocking   Technique to identify blocking assignment.

one-on-one   Creating, usually through motion, a man-to-man pass defense.

on side   Refers to the play side of the field (also frontside).

open step   Quarterback action directly toward the play.

option   Run whereby the defensive end is "optioned" instead of blocked.

out route   Pass route toward the sideline.

overload   Both slotbacks aligned on the same side prior to the snap.

over stride   Quarterback takes too big a stride when throwing the football, which usually results in a low throw.

PAT   Point after touchdown.

patterns   A group of routes to form a pattern.

pitch   Refers to quarterback action on the option or pitch play, tossing the ball to a back, usually underhanded.

pitch man   The back who is in position to receive the pitch from the quarterback.

pitch relationship   The proper distance between back and quarterback.

play action   Action of the backfield during a given play.

play book   Written offensive or defensive plays for players to study.

point of attack   The point whereby the football will attack the defense.

pre-snap read   Quarterback surveying the defensive alignment prior to the snap of the football.

primary receiver   Receiver within a pattern thought to be the first option in the play.

pulling   An offensive lineman backing off the line of scrimmage on the snap of the football to lead the ball carrier.

quarterback   Player behind center.

quick screen   Screen pass to the fullback to the outside.

reach block   Blocking a player aligned to the offensive blocker's outside.

read option route   Refers to giving the receiver the option of one route or another depending on the action of the defensive after the snap of the ball.

receiver   Play to whom the pass is designed to go.

red   Short motion by the left slotback.

reverse pivot   Quarterback action initially away from the play.

ride   Refers to the quarterback and fullback action on the veer or belly play.

rip   Medium motion by the left slotback crossing the formation.

roar   Long motion by the left slotback.

rotating safety   Defensive safety reacting to motion by moving toward the motion prior to the snap.

route   An individual action by a receiver.

running backs   Fullback, slotbacks, or halfbacks.

scissors   Misdirection running play with an inside handoff by the quarterback to the slotback.

scramble route   An individual route whereby the receiver can run any route, on a four-count, away from the defensive back.

scrape stunt   Defensive action by the noseguard and the backside linebacker, crossing after the snap of the football.

screen   Pass play behind the line of scrimmage after allowing the defensive line to rush the passer.

seal block   Blocking the perimeter to the inside.

seam   The area in a zone defense between the areas of defense.

seam-post route   Deep route between the safety and the corner backs.

secondary   Defensive players aligned in the defensive backfield.

sequence   Refers to the quarterback order of receivers to look at on a given pass play.

short   A scramble route with a three-count action point.

sink   Refers to the quarterback putting the football into the belly of the fullback on the veer play.

slant   A forty-five-degree line charge to the inside by the defensive line after the snap.

slant route   A pass route by a split receiver to the inside at approximately a five-yard depth.

slotback   Position of the offensive back one yard outside and one yard behind the offensive tackle.

slot key   Refers to the defensive player that the slotback keys on to determine his action on a given play.

slots-cross pattern   Goal line pattern whereby the slot-backs cross at approximately a ten-yard depth.

slow screen   Screen pass with a four-count.

soft corner   Refers to the defensive action on the perimeter of the defense.

speed cut   Fast cut by the split receiver on the sting pattern.

speed screen   Screen pass to the split receiver.

split defense   Defensive position with two linebackers aligned in the middle of the defensive formation.

split end   Refers to the wide receiver.

sprint out   Action by the quarterback to the outside, usually to avoid a strong inside defensive rush.

stack defense   Any defense with the linebackers directly behind a defensive lineman.

stalk-block   Technique used by split receivers and backs to block defensive backs.

stance   The body position of a given player prior to the snap.

Stanford pattern   A quick screen with buck action by the fullback.

stationary slotback   Slotback not in motion prior to the snap.

sting   Pattern most frequently used by the offense in the pass game.

stretching the secondary   Refers to deep routes used to stretch the distance the defense has to cover.

strong safety blitz   The strong safety attacking across the line of scrimmage after the snap of the ball.

student body right   Sweep play made famous by the University of Southern California.

stunts   Action by the defensive line other than a straight-ahead charge.

sucker block   Action whereby the offensive blocker fakes a pass-block drop to entice the defensive lineman across the line of scrimmage.

surface block   Refers to the technique used in the one-on-one block.

sweep   Wide running play designed to get outside the defense.

swing block   Refers to an uncovered lineman looping to the outside and meeting a linebacker at the point of attack.

switch pattern   A combination pattern between the slotback and the split receiver crossing and running deep routes.

terminology   Refers to the language used to describe offensive or defensive plays, motions, cadence, etc.

three-deep secondary   Refers to a zone defensive scheme with three players assigned to the deep zones.

three-point stance   Offensive position with one hand on the ground.

three-step drop   Quarterback action used in the short passing game.

throwback   Quarterback sprinting to one side and throwing back to the opposite side.

thuds   Team action at full speed with no tackling.

tight end   A slotback aligned on the line of scrimmage.

toe-in   Refers to quarterback footwork, turning foot toward the midline or center of the body.

toe-out   Refers to quarterback footwork, turning foot away from the midline or center of the body.

touchdown pattern   Combination pattern with clear out route by slotback and cross by split receiver.

trap   Blocking scheme by linemen.

twins   Formation adjustment with slotback aligned outside the split receiver.

two-step drop   Quick pass footwork by the quarterback.

under coverage   Refers to the linebacker positioning in the pass defense.

up route   Also called *fade*. Deep route by individual receiver.

veer   Fullback inside play with an option by the quarterback to give or keep depending on action of the defense.

wham   Long motion by the right slotback.

white   Short motion by the right slotback.

wide   Refers to an alignment of the slotback halfway between the split receiver and the tackle.

wiz   Medium motion across the backfield by the right slotback.

you block   Cross block between the guard and tackle with the guard going first.

zip   Motion by the flanker. Used in the 800 formation.

zone block   Refers to the linemen blocking a zone rather than a man. Usually used against a stack defense.

zone defense   Refers to the secondary play in pass defense.

About the Author

One of the most successful football coaches in the nation, Tom Smythe is known for his imaginative approach to offense— from his 22-year career as a head coach in AA and AAA high schools to his time as an assistant coach with Oregon State University and the USFL's Portland Breakers. His teams are perennial leaders in pass offense and scoring, averaging 31.3 points per game. Tom's high school coaching record is 156-32-1, making him one of the five "winningest" coaches in Oregon football history. Tom also garnered a 3-1 record for the times he served as head coach of the Oregon Shrine All-Star games.

After a successful 17-year stint at Lakeridge High School in Lake Oswego, Oregon, Tom is now head football coach for Lewis & Clark College, where he earned an MA in education in 1970. In his leisure time, Tom enjoys playing golf and traveling with his wife, Nancy. He has combined his love of golf and travel in his book *On and Off the Fairways: In the British Isles.*